choosing happiness

Also by Alexandra Stoddard

choosing happiness

keys to a joyful life

ALEXANDRA STODDARD

Collins
An Imprint of HarperCollinsPublishers

To *Peter, Alexandra,* and *Brooke:*

Your energy is pure light,

pure love, pure joy.

You know the secret of

"Love & Live Happy."

HarperCollins books may be purchased for educational, business, or sales promotional use. For information, please write to: Special Markets Department, HarperCollins Publishers, 10 East 53rd Street, New York, New York 10022.

FIRST COLLINS EDITION 2006.

Designed by Marysarah Quinn

Library of Congress Cataloging-in-Publication Data is available upon request.

Stoddard, Alexandra.
Choosing happiness : keys to a joyful life /
Alexandra Stoddard.—1st ed.
p.   cm.
ISBN-10: 0-06-000804-0
ISBN-13: 978-0-06-000804-8
1. Happiness.   I. Title.

BF575.H27 S76   2002
170'.44—dc21
2001039674

06 07 08 09 10 RRD 20 19 18 17 16 15 14

I acknowledge you with admiration, appreciation, and love:

To my literary agent Carl Brandt: In our fifth decade together, your vision, wisdom, intuition, and intelligent guidance continue to inspire my best thoughts, my happiest power. Bless you for believing in me when I was a young writer struggling and eager to publish my thoughts.

Thank you for your knowledge about how to reshape this manuscript on the ultimate subject, happiness.

To my editor, Toni Sciarra: We have been together for nine books. I value your brilliant work, your insights, and the depth you bring to my writing. Having you continue to be my editor at HarperCollins is a grace note of happiness.

I have tried to get my arms around the elusive subject of happiness. Thank you for sticking by me. Your help is invaluable.

To my friends and readers: Your loving kindness, support, encouragement, and input in helping me to research and search for universal truths about happiness are deeply appreciated. I hope you will feel this book sheds light on your own happiness.

To Sharon Scarpa: You are an angel. We've been together for two previous books, with me writing longhand and you doing your magic on the computer. Your loyalty as I wrote this book, rewrote, re-cast, and finally completed it over five years is grace under fire. I am grateful.

contents

Love & Live Happy

happiness as the first principle of life

Twenty-eight years ago, when my first book was published—*Style for Living: How to Make Where You Live You*—I began touring to give talks and have continued to do so ever since. My exposure to people across the country over these years has given me the understanding that basically we all want the same thing—to be happy.

I have heard stories of love, loss, faith, hope, beauty, birth, family, home, friendship; and courage, from good people trying to live as well as humanly possible, often under trying circumstances.

Over the years happiness has emerged as the first principle of life. Happiness, universally, is thought to be the most desirable of all things. I wanted to learn more about this elusive subject. I studied scientific research and began asking my audiences and readers for their thoughts and experiences. I read widely among philosophers of various disciplines. This is what I learned: Happiness basically means well-being. It is always good, and always a choice. Happiness is not automatic but must be wisely pursued. We need to make the choice to be happy in a particular situation, just as it is, and at a given moment. It might not be a perfect moment but it is ours; we are breathing; we are alive. We choose our happiness incrementally, moment by moment, hour by hour. Now.

Choosing happiness over sadness, indifference, or misery forms a structure for our lives. Working toward the brighter side is also beneficial in all we think and do.

Cultivating the vital energy of mindfulness will keep us focused on happiness. We must pay attention to everything. Everything matters because everything is interconnected, the small with the big. The cell or seed is not small, because it is the foundation of what becomes big. A child grows up to become a world leader; an acorn becomes an oak tree.

Making happiness the first principle of our lives gives us direction and purpose, and so increases our energy. Feeling passionate about what we choose to do is central to happiness, bringing fresh richness to our lives that gives birth to new insights and more profound understanding. When we spend our lives using our gifts, we are playing our part in the human drama, the mysterious miracle of our being born and living now, and we gain a vibrancy, a love of life, to share with others.

Painful times can, paradoxically, deepen our love of life—if we remain focused on our commitment to choose happiness. We all know what unhappiness is and how it feels. What some people don't necessarily know is how to deal with it and move on. Unhappiness is real and has its place in healing. Often, we learn about happiness from being unhappy. We need strategies and tools to better cope with unhappiness, disappointment, and pain. We can train our minds not to become defined by unhappy circumstances beyond our control.

Happiness is subjective. We feel its energy and are conscious of it personally. Likewise, we are personally responsible for finding happiness through our choices and attitudes. I estimate that approximately half of the ways to increase our happiness can be derived from wise, imaginative choices. The other half comes from our willingness to accept whatever happens, to make the necessary adjustments and move forward.

The events of September 11, 2001, profoundly and permanently changed all of our lives. Catastrophic occurences such as these terrorist attacks have the power to overwhelm us with grief, fear, and even rage. But eventually thay can make us stronger, raise our consciousness, and awaken us to reality. We're summoned to call forth our full talents and resources of time, energy, money, love, and care.

Our inner and collective resources are being challenged in a fundamental way, as has the concept that happiness can be a choice. For me, the crushing devastation intermingled with the purest miracle—my first-born child Alexandra giving birth to perfectly healthy twins, recipients, I can bear witness, of unconditional love.

Somehow, these two polar energies—light and dark, happiness and sadness, creation and destruction, love and hate—placed me in a balanced perspective between optimism, faith, hope, and love, while at the same time being confronted by the darkest choices human beings can conceive, plan, and carry out against innocent men, women, and children. These earth-shaking events reinforced my already passionate belief that world peace begins with each person's inner peace and happiness.

We heal through becoming more interconnected, through small acts of loving kindness, through our quiet courage and heroism. We will not merely cope during difficulties and tragedies, we will grow in deeper compassion and love. Our vulnerability will be our strength.

We as individuals cannot change the universal condition.

What we can control is our attitude about life. I believe that we can be happy and positive even though objectively we often have valid reasons to be sad. True happiness is transcendent. Its grace is there to sustain us in all circumstances.

We are not alone in the ultimate quest. Let us choose happiness together. We can rise above the difficulties that are not within our control. No matter how sorrowful situations can be, we can still find meaning and purpose in life, with faith that life is a beautiful blessing.

I hope my book will give you insight, inspiration, and the necessary tools to help you live the rest of your life in a more joyful consciousness while remaining sensitive to the pain and sorrows of the world. Together we can smile through our tears, love each other more deeply, be kinder, more tender, and more caring. Choosing happiness for ourselves and wishing to spread joy to others is the healthiest, wisest, and most noble way to live our lives. I believe we can spread our inner light far and wide in a troubled world.

Happiness is the first principle of life.

Alexandra Stoddard

the happiness habit

—enjoying those things for which we were presumably designed in the first place . . . the opportunity to do good work, to fall in love, to enjoy friends, to sit under trees, to read, to hit a ball, to bounce a baby.

—ALISTAIR COOKE

happiness now

mindfulness is key

I've found that most people don't really think about happiness in a structured way. This is unfortunate, because by studying happiness, examining ourselves, and taking action based on our thinking, we can vastly improve our happiness. Of course, doing so requires necessary effort and focused discipline, if we are to sustain a long happiness. Happiness must become a habit, a way of looking at and appreciating life, the door we are always opening to let in more light and richer experiences.

How can we harness our rational mind for greater happiness? The first requirement of attaining happiness is a nurtured and culti-vated mindfulness. By developing the capacity to be fully present in each moment, we will live a life of greater depth and meaning, in

Here, now, always—
Quick now, here,
now, always

T. S. ELLIOT

> *One must put all the happiness one can into each moment.*
>
> EDITH WHARTON

touch with what is most beautiful in our true nature. We can train ourselves to be awake here and now, right in the thick of things, where we immediately and directly encounter the fullness and complexities of life.

Mindfulness keeps us grounded, in effect, similar to the pull of gravity. Our mindfulness skills need to be developed systematically, through daily practice, by our doing ordinary things wherever we are. We train our minds to concentrate our full attention on the present moment. Simply being aware of the wonderful things that are happening in our lives now greatly increases our happiness.

Awaken all your senses to each fresh experience. There should be no hierarchy of mindful moments. When we pay attention to the reality of this moment, and the next, and the next, we have a great deal more enjoyment. Seeing a little girl in a pink coat and hat headed off to a birthday party with a gift in her hands makes us feel good. Bumping into a friend on the street and stopping for a chat at a nearby coffeehouse gives us a lift. Sitting at the kitchen table in our bathrobe and slippers, reading the Sunday paper with

> *I always try to check my motivation and be mindful and present in the moment.*
>
> DALAI LAMA

sunlight flooding in the clean windows and illuminating the blue pitcher of daffodils is a treat. Making a delicious breakfast for the family comforts us. Lighting a fire enhances our evening reading. Helping a child learn to play basketball makes us feel nine years old again. Going for a sunset sail with your spouse stops the clock from ticking. Doing grocery shopping together reminds us we're glad to share each other's company, whatever we may be doing. Simple, everyday activities are where happiness thrives.

Life is not to be found anywhere else but in the present moment. We live to the hilt right here where we are, right now.

Mindfulness is a simple, practical way to absorb as much vitality, understanding, and sensitivity as possible out of the smallest details of our lives. Nothing we do is merely a means to an end. Glancing at the sky as you hurry home from work and noticing a magnificent cloud formation; seeing that someone took the time to plant bright red geraniums in their apartment window box; appreciating a particularly stalwart tree during an evening walk in your neighborhood or the indomitable forsythia that always finds a way to bloom no matter how harsh the winter; smiling at the chartreuse beauty of dozens of Granny Smith apples stacked in the supermarket produce section—these uplifting, mindful moments are available to us, hidden in our daily routines. When we practice mindfulness, we raise our consciousness to touch the wonders of life for self-nourishment, refreshment, and healing.

Moments big as years! (O moments big as years!)

JOHN KEATS

When we illuminate a favorite painting, we're immediately uplifted, and so is the artist's work. If we see that the shades on the bedroom swing-arm lamps are old and dingy, they can easily be replaced with some new white shades that will freshen the look of the whole room. Often, it is a simple, inexpensive improvement that gives us a big uplift.

When we walk on a pretty tree-lined street on a spring morning and experience the sunlight dappling the leaves, we immediately feel more sublime. The benefits of the experience linger as we move throughout the day. Paying

The U.S. Constitution doesn't guarantee happiness, only the pursuit of it. You have to catch up with it yourself.

BENJAMIN FRANKLIN

> *The ability to be in the present moment is a major component of mental wellness.*
>
> ABRAHAM MASLOW

attention to the smallest things will have a great cumulative impact on our overall sense of well-being. If we feel a surge of pleasure when we discover a new color of ink for our fountain pens while browsing in a beautifully appointed stationery store, we may decide to splurge and buy a box of pretty notepaper that will inspire us to write to friends. One good move informs another.

Caring deeply about the details of all the aspects of our lives magnifies our pleasurable experiences. Open your heart and your senses to the small things that add grace, ease, and harmony to your living experience now. Never underestimate, for example, the positive influence of carefully arranging our favorite books in a logical fashion on our library shelves. Or of organizing our CDs in labeled boxes. Who is to say how much happiness a new saucepan can bring, or a new pale yellow silk scarf to tuck in a blazer pocket, or a fresh bar of lemon soap for the kitchen sink?

Polishing a brass watering can, waxing an antique French provincial table, mending a favorite broken dish, framing pic-

> *Each moment presents what happens.*
>
> JOHN CAGE

tures of our families, having a favorite fountain pen repaired, organizing our writing desk, putting all our notecards, stationery, and postcards in an attractive box—anything we do with care becomes a pleasure and a path to happiness now.

Many experiences are inherently pleasant. We have—if we are very lucky—personal control over our immediate lives.

Surely, the saddest words in the English language are: "What might have been." We must not wait to awaken to the exuberant possibilities of life now. Life should be lived fully and lived well in all circumstances as best we can live it, and the time is now. Mindfulness is key.

beauty of the everyday

When we are awake to the full potential of each moment, nothing is ever routine. Everything seems fresh and inspiring because we're experiencing life on a higher awareness level. We awaken our five senses to new appreciation; we're more aware of the opportunities to enjoy everything we do. Our minds become pure, nourished with positive affirmative energy.

Every situation—no, every moment—is of infinite worth; for it is the representative of a whole eternity.

GOETHE

Living mindfully puts us in touch with the beauty of the most simple and common things. The ordinary is bathed in light, and we see and feel the extraordinary pleasure of having breakfast, taking a shower, washing our hair, doing dishes, knitting, ironing, shoveling snow from the front steps, walking to a meeting, sitting at our desks, shopping for fun, playing tennis, meeting a friend for tea, or watering the plants. We know firsthand that our domestic landscape is a song, a poem, a beautiful place that not only shelters us but brings us pleasure and a great deal of joy.

The Impressionists will always be admired for helping us to see that what we already have here and now is beautiful, full of light and color. What they did, we also do. We all share common rituals of eating, sleeping, and bathing. When we mindfully absorb ourselves in what we do, we feel we're inside a painting; like the Impressionists a century or more ago, we sense the sweetness of our own lives.

observe the hidden beauty

When we mindfully pay attention to the most humble moments, we feel their profound, often hidden, beauty. When we concentrate fully on the task at hand, we experience the sublime in our everyday activities. The next time you perform necessary tasks, give each one your undivided attention. You will see, within a few weeks, how much more energy and inner peace you will feel.

Write it on your heart that every day is the best day in the year.

EMERSON

Practice mindfulness when you iron napkins, open the mail, clean the oven, pay bills, put your feet up on an ottoman, bake bread, wash the car, polish the brass, clean curtains, wrap a gift, paint a coffee table, wash windows, feed the cat, repot a plant, organize files, write a postcard, walk the dog, plant seeds in the soil, or mow the lawn.

little things matter

Nothing is wholly insignificant. When I tend to the small things in a conscious way, the big things have a tendency to take care of themselves. A great deal of unhappiness is caused by the repeated accumulation of irritating little details that dampen our spirit. If I don't file my nails, I will probably run my new pair of stockings. If I don't tighten a loose button on a coat, it may fall off and I may lose it and not have another one that matches. The care and maintenance that we put into our immediate physical environment, our homes, our gardens, our possessions, our clothes, will always add to our sense of well-being and inner peace.

the past is over

Present-minded consciousness means that happiness is now. I love flowers and I must have them around me now. Not only can I enjoy them in my home but I can experience them in gardens along the road. I can visit botanical gardens. Today I can have my nose up against some primroses or daffodils, tulips or lilies. I'll find a way, because flowers make me happy.

Many people are preoccupied with the past or dream of the future, discounting now, the only place where they can enjoy the vital energy of the present. You and I have no control over the past. Whether the past is reflected upon as the good old days or as a time of disappointment and suffering, nothing can be changed or improved. The past is dead, gone forever, only to be retrieved in memories, films, scrapbooks, and memorabilia. The past, whether good or bad, is not where we should water the seeds of our consciousness, because doing so drains our energy from what is alive

To be alive, to be able to see, to walk, to have houses, music, paintings—it's all a miracle.

ARTHUR RUBINSTEIN

True happiness is to . . . enjoy the present, without anxious dependence upon the future.

SENECA

in us and around us now. Dwelling on the past inhibits our ability to move forward and take action to inspire our well-being. However we perceive the past, whether in a positive or negative light, concentrating on it makes us unhappier in the present. The past is past.

Through deliberate present-minded focus we can breathe in new life, new positive energy, letting go of the way things were in the past. When we grow more mindful, we open our hearts to forgiveness and choose not to get bogged down in placing blame or getting even with others. When we let go of the past, we gain in wisdom. We feel lighter and brighter, inspired by what we've learned, ready to move on.

Being sentimental, however, and remembering nostalgic moments, can temporarily help us to heal. After my brother Powell died in Chicago while having open-heart surgery, I was comforted by looking through my parents' scrapbooks to revisit our childhood photographs. I saw the blessings of my having had him as my older brother, a protector, supporter, and friend. Looking at the pictures helped me to grieve and move forward.

don't plan it, live it

Just as our energy cannot go backward, we cannot fast-forward time, either. The future has not yet been born. There is no guarantee that it ever will be. "Foreseeable" is a shaky prediction. Many people worry about future problems that may never happen. Others endlessly plan their life away. We can't become fully conscious except in the true reality of now.

What we have in this present moment is all we have. When we accept and live in present circumstances, we can remain positive and not judge what is happening. Wishing for now to be over or different, or hoping for a better outcome, takes our focus away from this living, present experience. None of us knows for sure what our future holds. Rather than dreaming about the future, we can bring ourselves back to life's pleasures now. Here we can have vitally direct experience with reality, what is actually happening. We can appreciate what is wonderful now. We can deliberately expose ourselves to all the pleasures available to us—the beauty of the sky, the clouds, birds in flight, trees, grass, flowers, animals, the ocean, stars, sun and moon, the miracle of being alive.

Magical things happen every day, if we allow it. Think of daylight, of the stars at night, a flower. A dandelion is a miracle.

PAMELA TRAVERS

Not long ago my cousin Russell came for a visit. She owns an independent bookstore in Charlottesville, Virginia. We were talking about happiness. She laughed when she remembered a French friend explaining to her that "You Americans have an obsession with happiness. You think about it, plan for it, and work toward it. We French find happiness making a celebration of dinner, sitting with a friend having coffee at a café, or meeting for lunch. We don't plan it, we live it."

We can set goals for ourselves, make plans for the future, and have a wish list. But the desire for a bigger house with a fenced-in yard, a larger apartment, or a downstairs powder room may never be realized. Live it up now.

Whenever we do anything well, when we do our best, embracing an activity wholeheartedly, we are satisfied and energized. Tucking a child into bed and saying a prayer after reading a story is a small act of grace with lasting benefits. Rituals can never be rushed or be skipped. The joy is in our instantaneous recognition of miraculous present moments.

Don't plan it. Live it.

spinning out of control

When we're spinning too fast and our mind is a muddle of negative distracting thoughts, we make mistakes. Not only do we become frustrated but we can cause harm to others and ourselves. We should remember to buckle up, to look both ways when we cross the street, and to focus on driving when we're behind the wheel of a car. Often the obvious escapes our consciousness.

Years ago, I was thinking about a book I was writing on color while I was driving home with Peter from the office in New York City in a hurricane. I took a left-hand turn without putting on my signal light or checking the outside mirror. There was zero visibility, and I didn't see any traffic. My mindless act caused a frightening accident when a taxi rushing alongside smashed into my Audi. Miraculously, Peter and I were not hurt, nor was the driver of the taxi, but our car was a total loss.

All moments are key moments, and life itself is grace.

FREDERICK BUECHNER

Recently, I went to a coffee shop and asked for a package of strong decaffeinated coffee. I served it to friends after dinner, assuring them it was decaffeinated. We sipped away the evening.

We were having so much fun no one wanted to leave. Not only did I sleep badly that night but I also had caffeine poisoning, an extremely toxic condition, worsened because I drank more of the same coffee the next morning, still unaware that the coffee contained caffeine. As it happened, the young man who sold me the coffee had mistakenly given me strong after-dinner coffee that contained caffeine.

The root is man, here and not there, now and not then.

DWIGHT MACDONALD

People will make mistakes, but it is our responsibility to follow up on the things we can control. If I had been more mindful, I would have noticed the package of coffee was not labelled "decaffeinated." By not being careful, I caused myself physical discomfort and unnecessary suffering. Even if no one is harmed, when we are mindless we do things that can be extremely inconvenient and make us feel foolish. If we go to the airport with our tickets but forget our passport or photo identification, we won't be able to board the plane. If we dash out for a lunch date and forget our wallet, we will feel discombobulated and embarrassed at not being able to pay.

On the afternoon after Powell died, Peter and I went to his home to be with his wife, children, grandchildren, and other family members. I inadvertently left my tote bag containing the original and only manuscript of *The Art of the Possible* on a wing chair in the hotel lobby, completely oblivious to this fact until the next day. Fortunately, the hotel found it and sent it to me in New York. When we go through a difficult situation, we should concentrate even more intensely on our breathing, being mindful of our every move.

By and by never comes.

SAINT AUGUSTINE

We all have painful stories of our being mindless. When I was a young bride I invited

How to gain, how to keep, how to recover happiness is . . . for most people at all times the secret motive of all they do.

WILLIAM JAMES

The highest possible stage in moral culture is when we recognize that we ought to control our thoughts.

CHARLES DARWIN

my in-laws to dinner. In my eagerness to have the roast beef perfectly timed so that it didn't become overdone, I decided not to put it in the oven until after the guests arrived. When it was time to sit down to dinner, I realized—woe—I'd neglected to put the roast in the preheated oven after all!

Once I was driving home from Connecticut, briefly lost my mindfulness, missed the turn to Manhattan, and ended up in Long Island. The consequences were no more than time-consuming and disturbing, but it could have been dangerous being lost alone in the dark.

When we are scattered, we often repeat the same mistake several times. We dial the wrong number and somehow do it a second time. I have an uncomfortable memory of making a lemon dessert and three times putting the sugar in with the yolks instead of the whites, each time having to start over from scratch, becoming more agitated as it came closer to the time guests were to arrive for dinner.

How many times have we forgotten a crucial birthday? Thinking about it ahead of time is not the same as giving a gift or acknowledging it in some way. When we are mindful, these slip-ups don't occur as often.

I regret any time I've been insensitive and let words pop out of my mouth that could hurt someone's feelings. I remember laughing about how "I can't cope with taupe" to an audience filled with women wearing taupe pants suits. It was a sea of taupe! I could easily have avoided my careless mistake if I had focused on all the details of my audience, not just their faces.

We lock car keys in the car. We lock our-selves out of the house or apartment. We go to Italy and if we're not mindful we give a taxi driver seventy dollars instead of seven because we didn't concentrate on the lira exchange rate. When we get to the bottom of the popcorn bowl, we can't mindlessly bite into the unpopped kernels without the risk of cracking a tooth. If we forgot and leave the dishwasher door open and go to the stove or refrigerator, we may gash our leg—and sometimes painfully do.

> *We can go through our whole lives worrying about our future happiness, and totally miss where true peace lives—right here, right now.*
>
> PETER RUSSELL

I once mindlessly put a fountain pen in a jacket pocket rather than in a pen case in my purse. The pink ink leaked, per-manently damaging a favorite apple-green silk jacket. I've learned my lesson, but it still stings to remember my careless-ness. And if you've ever left your credit card at a restaurant, you realize how dumb you can feel over such an innocent mistake, especially after strange charges appear on your statement the following month. Whenever we leave to go on a lecture tour, Peter says, "glasses, passports, tickets, slides, notes." Maybe that is one of the roles of a companion: *to remind us to think.* I have a friend who tapes a list to the front door: $, TICKETS/ID, GLASSES, LOCK UP, GARBAGE, CAT CARE NOTE, COFFEE MACHINE OFF!

concentration leads to insight

Whatever we do, when we have good intentions and make our best effort, there is goodness. Think about a chore that you do not enjoy doing. Now, challenge yourself to think about it as a grace note of happiness. How many such tasks come to mind? Perhaps you don't like emptying the garbage. Focus on the garbage intensely. You might have an idea about setting up a compost bin in your backyard to enrich the soil for your vegetable garden. This idea could further lead to discernment that you are really longing for a pretty flower garden in front of the house. Or perhaps you'll find a more efficient or aesthetic method that streamlines the task and makes it more pleasant.

Life, we learn too late, is in the living, in the tissue of every day and hour.

STEPHEN LEACOCK

While cleaning the wood floor in your entrance hall, you envision a pretty sea-foam green you may paint on the walls because that color always makes you smile by reminding you of sunny island beaches. Doing your chores while listening to a favorite piano CD makes you realize that you should collect more instrumental music to play throughout the day and evening at home, because music expands your heart.

By looking in a full-length mirror as you dress, you see that your clothes are too tight and you need to be more mindful of your diet, consciously eating more vegetables and fruit, eating more slowly. As you brush your hair, you realize you should make an appointment to have it trimmed. As you reach for a mug for your morning coffee, is there a pretty one that gives you pleasure? Are there some ugly clunkers you would be happy to throw out to make space for more attractive ones? When you see the sunlight on a favorite chair where you like to read, and you see the chintz looks tired, either have it cleaned or consider having it recovered

Let us savor the most fleeting delights of our most beautiful day.

ALPHONSE DE

LAMARTINE

in a fresh, colorful chintz. Try to use whatever you concentrate on as a way to become more sensitive and discerning. Whenever possible, grasp the inward or hidden lessons in things.

Nine-tenths of wisdom consists in being wise in time.

THEODORE ROOSEVELT

awakening in the garden

I first learned about mindfulness when I was three years old and awoke to consciousness of beauty in my mother's flower garden. In the years since then, I have learned that to the degree I can stay focused and concentrate on what is happening in me and around me, I have kept some of the sense of wonder I experienced that July morning as an innocent child. Because of my profound awakening, I am ever mindful of my hunger and deep-seated need to envelop myself in nature's beauty. I am not alone.

our vital base

Draw an equilateral triangle on a piece of paper. In the bottom left-hand corner of the triangle, write "mindfulness." In the bottom right-hand corner, write *self-awareness*. These are the two pillars of our vital base for greater happiness and a richer, deeper, and more meaningful life. Whenever we are in the energy flow of mindfulness, we dramatically increase our intuitive nature.

Act well at the moment, and you have performed a good action to all eternity.

JOHANN KASPAR

LAVATER

It is never selfish to be mindful. Until we are mindful and knowledgeable about our bodies,

All men seek happiness. This is without exception. Whatever different means they employ, they all tend to this end.

BLAISE PASCAL

our thoughts, and our emotions, including our fears and desires, we cannot be complete. We don't stand a chance of becoming a whole, authentic, well-adjusted, happy person until we acknowledge that everything in our life matters. We know what is true and beautiful when we learn from our own direct experience. Paradoxically, we can then broaden our perspective, seeing things from a more universal point of view, because we're in tune with life as it is really happening. We deserve to be happy. We are as much a part of this universe as billion-year-old stars, ancient trees, the oceans, and the sky. We are an integral part of the harmony of the cosmos.

We should aspire to live up to our happier higher power. I've come to realize that when we are happy, we are in touch with our greatest human potential. There is only one you and only one me on this planet. If we don't play our own parts, no one else can substitute for us, because our talents and gifts are ours alone.

The happiest person is the person who thinks the most interesting thoughts.

WILLIAM LYON PHELPS

We must pay attention to our vital base, always asking ourselves, "Is this me?" "Is this what I really feel?" "Is this what I truly believe?" "Is what I'm doing increasing my sense of happiness?" "Are my thoughts and feelings spreading light and joy to myself and others?" Often our sense of pleasure and joy comes from our private enthusiasms, our taking time to care and nourish what we love to do, not merely from the big job bringing big pay, or things that are socially visible. Rather, our happiness builds when we do things that make us feel passionately alive.

Many people tell me their passions, often enjoyed simply for their own fulfillment. You don't have to be a great musician to work hard at music. You can play in a marching band or sing in a church choir. Often you do what you do because there's fun and joy in what you passionately pursue, not because of financial rewards. We have to go for it, do what makes our juices flow now. We should do what fulfills us even if we are not paid to do it. We don't have to be a great gardener to love to dig in the soil. We don't have to get paid to nurture unwanted children as foster parents.

Remember this, that very little is needed to make a happy life.

MARCUS AURELIUS

From our vital base of mindfulness and self-awareness, the triangle rises to form an apex. Let that peak be the unique light of your true nature shining through you.

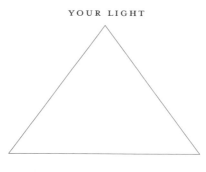

YOUR LIGHT

MINDFULNESS

SELF-AWARENESS

hurry never

I learned a great deal about fully enjoying the moment from my friend, boss, and mentor, Eleanor McMillen Brown. Mrs. Brown was born in 1890 and died five days shy of her one hundred first

One must learn to husband time carefully, in order to enjoy life in the here and now.

MIHALY

CSIKSZENTMIHALYI

birthday. Her famous advice to the designers who were devoted to her and her firm: "If you create beauty for your own life, if you create beauty for other people's lives, you will live a long, healthy, happy life." Mrs. Brown never rushed. She was organized, disciplined, and available to fully appreciate each experience as it unfolded before her. I was fifty-three years her junior, honored to work at her side and experience close up how much love, care, and thoughtfulness went into everything she said and did. As an interior designer, she taught us that we should develop our talent and skill to always make things more beautiful, more harmonious, more cheerful and charming.

Because Mrs. Brown celebrated her life in a civilized and intelligent manner, she was an extraordinary inspiration, teacher, and role model. By her example, she trained hundreds of interior designers not just about style and taste but about the value of living well. Each of us, in turn, in our own way, tries to continue to spread her influence and remember her lesson.

don't save time—lose it

America is the last great experiment for human happiness.

GEORGE WASHINGTON

We live in an age of multi-tasking, trying to do many things at once to save time. We all are guilty of overburdening our schedules and minds. However, our brain is not structured like a computer. We can't actually do two things at once. Journalist Catherine Bush wrote recently in a *New York Times* article that the actions we perform—even the simplest ones—are done in a "strict linear sequence." Multi-tasking, she says, is actually task switching. The brain time-shares. Studies show that if we try to do two things at once, "the brain stalls fractionally before responding to the second stimulus." When seconds matter, we are better off not doing another task. We all do mental juggling, but when we prioritize what tasks we must perform, we're able to immerse ourselves in what we do. Whenever we try to do too much in too little time, we are less effective and don't do anything well. When we squeeze the pleasure out of the living moment with the distractions of multi-tasking, we have lost the fun and spirit of the process moment to moment.

> *Come to me . . . and let us be as happy as we can.*
>
> SAMUEL JOHNSON

There is always time to do what is important. I saw a little girl in a restaurant recently, using a spoon to imitate her mother, who was next to her, talking on a cellular telephone, not paying any attention to her daughter. Being fully present when we're with a child, looking into their sparkling eyes, is love made visible. Seeing their simplicity and innocence, we become open to every wonder, creating timeless, priceless moments.

The joy is always in being completely absorbed in whatever we are doing. What are some of your favorite activities that cause you to lose all sense of time? Some examples of my own come to mind: walking on a deserted beach, writing a letter to a child, playing with a

> *My time is today.*
>
> GEORGE GERSHWIN

baby, sitting by a fire, writing in a journal, playing the piano, walking in a garden or park, dancing to favorite music, having dinner with friends, seeing a favorite old movie, appreciating the "now moments." Happiness can become a habit. When it does, we can attain endless joy.

CHAPTER 2

who am i?

What is your purpose, what is your calling? What I know for sure is, if you ask
the question the answer will come. What I
know for sure is, you have to be willing to
listen for the answer. You have to get still
enough to learn it and hear it and pay
attention, to be fully conscious enough
to see not just with your eyes but through
them to the truth of who you are and
what you can be.

—OPRAH WINFREY

know yourself

The only way to obtain lasting happiness is to acquire self-knowledge through regularly looking inward. We are trained not to be self-oriented. We've been taught since birth not to think of ourselves. I believe that self-denial and selflessness have gone too far. There are inherent dangers in lack of self-regard, because if we don't think highly of ourselves, it will be difficult for us to value others. We seem to have some inhibition about freely expressing our strengths and talents even to ourselves. It's not part of our culture. If we are aware of our good points, however, we often can develop the courage to deal with and correct our weaknesses.

The best way is to understand yourself, and then you will understand everything.

SHUNRYN SUZUKI

When we know ourselves well, we're free to move forward with our lives, being true to our nature throughout all of life's changing chapters. Inner intelligence deepens our experiences and gives our life greater richness and meaning.

being led

The way to become more self-aware is to tap into our intuition, our inner guidance, for greater clarity and vision. Intuition is often called the sixth sense. Our intuition leads the way for our other five senses to teach us more about ourselves. Our discipline of mindfulness makes us more self-aware at all times, not just occasionally. Being open to listen and really hear the voice within is like turning on a searchlight in a dark room.

When we trust our inner consciousness, we let it color and flavor everything in our world. Self-awareness increases our self-confidence. Following our hunches leads to inner motivation.

The highest purpose of the human species is to justify the gift of life.

NORMAN COUSINS

We may not know why we have an impulse to take a detour. Recently I was in a taxi, coming home from downtown. I had an urge to get out at a stoplight and walk the rest of the way home. One reason was that I wanted the exercise, but there were many other unexpected rewards. I browsed in my favorite Swedish paper store on Madison Avenue and found several small spiral books that inspired me, because the covers can be changed to eight different colors, so I could change the color daily. I strolled up the street to a butcher shop and bought some chicken-veal burgers for a cozy dinner at home. I saw a banner at the Metropolitan Museum of Art and was drawn to see the show of the great Dutch master Vermeer. Once there, I bumped into a friend (coincidence?), and we ended up having tea together at a café. By the time I got home, I felt recharged. I had food for dinner as well as food for thought. The unscheduled detour had refreshed me.

Self-love is not only necessary and good, it is a prerequisite for loving others.

ROLLO MAY

Have you ever been drawn to enter an art gallery, there to discover a painting you love? I go into galleries with an open heart, hoping I'll fall in love with a painting. This adventure is always fun, whether the magic happens or not. No one hits the intuitive mark every time. Some of our detours are sure to surprise us, but they will always be valuable learning experiences. They're all interesting and informative in their own way. We cannot control what will happen, but we can follow the leads.

In a heavy rainstorm in Provence in 1963, I was forced to take shelter. I parked the car in front of an antiques store in Grasse, where I discovered, in the window, an antique table that drew me. My connection with the table was so powerful my heart pounded. I realized—and believe it even more all these years later—that certain things are meant to be. I was twenty-two years old, and I didn't need an antique table. But I listened to the truth in my heart. This table, purchased for $285, has been my favorite object. It is my high altar, a place I come to with awe and reverence. We somehow find ways of making these heart connections. These experiences are spontaneous and, yes, serendipitous. They just happen, and when we are awake, we hear the call.

> *This is the true joy in life, the being used for a purpose recognized by yourself as a mighty one.*
>
> GEORGE BERNARD SHAW

Not all of our instincts are self-serving. We often have powerful motivations to serve others in a host of altruistic ways. I know a restaurant owner who suddenly had an insight that he wasn't using his teaching talents. He came to the realization that he wanted to leave the restaurant business and teach inner-city children.

> *There is divine meaning in the life of the world, of man, of human persons, of you and of me.*
>
> MARTIN BUBER

Pay attention to your impulses. They will most often be sudden, unexpected, and surprising. When we remain mindful, we're not caught off guard. Look for the light on your path. If you're drawn to look at vibrant bolts of bright cotton fabric in a shop

window, ask yourself if you need more color in your surroundings. If you do, where? At home or at the office? Analyze your
impulses. Be available to the experience in order to draw it out
to be examined and considered. You don't necessarily have to
follow your leads, but be receptive to clues.

setting the scene

While insights and intuitive perceptions can and do come to us
any time and any place, we can encourage them at home. We set
the scene for inner illumination by protecting ourselves from
distractions. Sometimes we want to be alone and quiet.

Each of us will find our own place where we like to be alone.
The ambience is important. Choose a place that you love the
most, a spot where you feel your energy is
dominant. Whatever environment has the
most spirit of place for you, whatever shines
the most inward light, the better. I set the
scene at my writing table. For me, this is a
special place. I light a candle, have fresh flowers, and look at pictures by my artist friend
Roger Mühl. These paintings speak volumes
to me, creating an ambience that uplifts my mood.

*These moments that
arise out of depths can
never be expressed in
words.*

JOHN BOWEN

COBURN

The mere practice of going to my writing table regularly
awakens my feelings, opens my consciousness to deeper
rhythms of awareness. It is here that I experience timeless
moments, where I see favorite treasured objects up close—photographs of my children, books that nourish me, a few senti-

mental treasured gifts from loved ones, letters, stamps, stationery, my pens, ink, and pads of smooth white paper.

centering ourselves

I believe that we all need our own sacred space in our homes. A place we know is ours alone, not to be violated, where we generate wholesome karma. Some people have a favorite place that they regularly visit. I have a friend in Florida who sits on a terrace every morning to watch the sun rise. We can set the scene for reflective time anywhere—at the office or even in a hotel room. Be patient. Inner intelligence cannot be forced. All we really have to do is be present, be quiet, listen, and watch what is happening inside us.

your five intuitive words

Your inner sparks are full of rich surprises and are really a lot of fun. To be receptive to intuitive feelings, write down five words that you feel give you insight into your self right now. Do it fast, from your pure consciousness, so your ego won't interfere. Your words could be *exercise, peaceful, garden, sexy,* and *hungry,* or *lonely, energetic, light, travel,* and *colorful.*

> *Life is a pure flame, and we live by an invisible sun within us.*
>
> THOMAS BROUNE

Out of your five words, pick one that speaks most strongly to you. If you choose *garden,* it could be that you are starved to be out in nature, experiencing the wonders of spring after a cold, dark New England winter. You may decide to rearrange your garden, add some window boxes to bring the flowers to eye level when you're inside, or simply buy one plant to brighten a room. If you choose *peaceful,* it could mean that you have been traveling too much, spinning too fast, and you're hungry for quiet relaxation. If you choose *exercise,* it could be that you haven't been able to go to the gym, and you miss it. You could take a daily morning or evening walk, join a yoga class or, if it would be helpful, go to a physical therapist who can teach you how to move your body without harming yourself. If one of your words is *painting,* you might have the impulse to take up oil painting again, something you abandoned after your third child was born. If your big word is *water,* you could cultivate your intuition to think about living closer to the sea, vacationing there, or enjoying some inexpensive framed prints of seaside places.

Our real personality is all light, all love, always shining.

UPANISHADS

Some people believe that our capacity for happiness is genetic and does not depend on environmental factors. I disagree. We are all prompted, of course, by our natural temperamental tendencies. But if you are happiest when you are near water, could you consider a radical move from inland to a coastal region, if this is where you feel most at home? If you are a water person, you are probably drawn to take vacations near water. Even taking a bath or swimming in a pool could be happiness triggers for you.

Even the sun and stars borrow light from the light of consciousness. The Self shining.

SAINT TERESA

OF AVILA

This exercise of writing down five words can help keep you in close touch with your innate

personality. Doing the exercise, you may experience many
moments when your intuition flashes out of the blue. Use this
exercise of instant knowing whenever you get
the urge to be reflective. It is a quick, concrete
way to draw out insights without excessively
deep contemplation. This simple ritual may
trigger a thought about taking up a new project.
For example, once when one of my words was
order, I realized my closets were a wreck, with
things spilling out in all directions, making me feel anxious.

Light, even though it passes through pollution, is not polluted.

SAINT AUGUSTINE

Consider doing this exercise at least once a day. It shouldn't
take more than a minute. It will enhance and empower your
inner light and voice. What we cultivate in our consciousness is
what we will attract and manifest in our lives. Daily, ask yourself
if your intuitive words ring true to your immediate needs and
spirit.

ten defining words

In my book *Feeling at Home: Defining Who You Are and How You Want to
Live*, I asked readers to write down ten words that define who
they are. This suggestion arose from an insight of my daughter
Brooke, who lived in Paris after graduating from college. Sitting at a café, she wrote her ten words, and they have helped her
to be true to herself in her life choices.

When I wrote down the ten words that define who I am, I
saw clearly the answer to the question "Who am I?" as it related
to my attaining my own happiness. My own ten words are *love,
sunlight, gardens, beaches, children, food, family, color, ribbons,* and *home*.

Love

The first word, the central word in my life, is love. I am happy when I am in a loving consciousness. Like everyone else, I desire to love and be loved. We know and understand ourselves best by what we love. Who are the people you love? Where are the places you've traveled, near and far, beautiful spots on earth that speak to you, that have a spirit of place, that nourish you and inspire you? What animals are you most fond of? What do you love most to do to help others? What interests are you most passionate about?

Though we travel the world over to find the beautiful, we must carry it with us or we find it not.

EMERSON

When we love, our energy is light, shining brightly in all directions. By being available, really being present, to our direct experiences, we increase our loving energy, because we are one with what we are doing and feeling.

Sunlight

In the sunlight I open up like a flower, smiling. When I'm out in the bright sunshine I feel an inner calm, a contentment, a sense of the earth being kissed with grace. I thrive in the light, as we all do. Light to me is happy, and I make every effort to experience as much natural light as I can. After a rain, when the sun breaks through the clouds and I see those rays of divine light, my heart expands. I worship the sun, because it is our life force. We need it to live, and I need it to feel playful, young, and carefree. I skip, have a bounce in my step, and feel great exhilaration when the sun is shining.

Gardens

Since my early garden experience, I know I can always find comfort when I walk or sit in a garden. The garden is a magical place where I feel what is sacred in my everyday life. I can go to a garden, be still, and feel refreshed. Gardens have a powerful hold over me and are always a place of healing. There is such tenderness in flowers, such beauty and integrity. Flowers are a vital source of my happiness, helping to keep me centered, to be true to my own nature. Flowers remind me how beautiful and fragile life is. Consider the supreme dignity of a single flower.

Beaches

Another place of great joy for me is the beach. Ever since I was little, playing in the sand, running freely on the beach, swimming and diving, I've always found beaches to be restorative. I feel reborn, refreshed, and filled with a feeling of expansiveness as I soak in the fresh salt air, mingle with the water, and watch the waves clap to shore. The changing light, the ebb and flow of the tide, the different colors of blue and purple, speak to me in a rhythmic voice that makes me feel that I've come home.

> *The world is a looking glass and gives back to every man the reflection of his own face.*
>
> WILLIAM MAKEPEACE
>
> THACKERAY

Children

I love children tenderly. They are so fresh, so pure, so innocent. I love to be with them, to have them show me around, let me into their world, let me be open, whimsical, full of curiosity and intense delight in whatever we may be doing. Children don't admire an orchid more than a dandelion. They are not superficial. They teach us to keep the child alive in us, to be more spontaneous, to improvise more, to take our joy wherever we are. Children are our teachers. They make us laugh and let us play with them, and we feel new, fresh, and vibrantly alive in their presence.

Food

Food to me is love. I feel nourished, satisfied, strengthened, and delighted by a beautiful meal. I try to dine, not merely eat. I enjoy the ritual, the time away from obligations and deadlines. When I eat, I am mindful of the celebration. I appreciate the pretty china and crystal, the linens, candles, and flowers. The way food looks on a plate, as well as how it tastes, matters a great deal to me.

Self-reverence, self-knowledge, self-control; these three alone lead life to sovereign power.

ALFRED, LORD

TENNYSON

I am passionate about pretty tablecloths and colorful napkins, dishes, and glassware. As we nourish our bodies with the food we eat, the aesthetic dimension of breaking bread opens our hearts to enjoy meaningful conversations, to toast loved ones in an attractive setting, to open all our senses to their full strength. We tell stories, we share laughter, and we share tears. The meal becomes a blessing.

Food is necessary for our survival and is central to every celebration. I value the daily rituals of breakfast, lunch, teatime, and dinner, which make me fully present to the grace in each repast, as I feel restored and made new. I'm reminded that the origin of the word restaurant is *restaurer*, the French for "restore."

Family

I feel blessed to be a central part of a warm, loving family. We care about each other, and we do what we can to be helpful to each other. Our general mantra is that we do the best that we can. No one is perfect. We disagree and know pain, but overall our community is one of love and support. Family, in my research, ranks very high on the scale of happiness.

Being a parent is a great blessing. I've always put my children before all else. I chose to be their mother, and I feel honored and privileged to be their supporter, their cheer-leader, their biggest fan in all their triumphs, and to help out whenever needed. Parenthood brings happiness to a great many of us.

In our tight-knit family, we also embrace our extended families, our parents, our grandparents, and all our ancestors. The evolution and continuity of the cycle of human life and love is forever fascinating and forever fresh.

> *To have peace and confidence within our souls—these are the beliefs that make for happiness.*
>
> MAURICE
> MAETERLINCK

Color

Color speaks to me louder than form, louder than words. I can travel to foreign countries and without knowing the language, I can sense the energy, the spirit of the people through the colors I absorb. The colors that I love are fresh from nature's magic palette. The clear blues of the sky on a sunny day, the fresh blues of the ocean, the colors of all the trees, grass, blossoms, flowers, fruits, and vegetables resonate in me. Colors are literally wavelengths of energy. They are alive and touch me deeply. Colors resound. I am inspired by the nature that these colors represent. They enlarge my imagination, my ability to appreciate and envision the beauty available to all of us if we reach out to see and experience this revelation of nature.

There will never be anything manufactured that is as beautiful as nature. All art imitates. What brings me great joy is to surround myself with nature, to select colors that have happy associations with the beauty I experience on a spring day when the sun shines, highlighting the world's freshness and luminescence. I am extremely sensitive to the nuances of color and know what a difference it makes to my spirit to be around sunny colors. We can increase our happiness enormously by becoming more aware of what colors make us feel good and what colors don't. Color plays a strong part in our sense of well-being.

> *I want to be all that I am capable of becoming.*
>
> KATHERINE MANSFIELD

Ribbons

I indulge in the joy of ribbons every day of my life. I love to wrap gifts. I can put a ribbon around a bar of soap and feel happier as I give it to a friend. I tuck ribbons in books as bookmarks. Wherever I travel, I always find a shop that sells ribbons where I can add to my collection. Like stationery, ribbons are always shared. We send them out to others. We tie packages in them; we put them in our daughter's hair. Ribbons always have joyful associations. They bring cheer, they hide surprises, and they are tactile, colorful, and exuberant. They bring us joyful moments and are always present at a happy celebration.

> *Bless the good-natured, for they bless everybody else.*
>
> THOMAS CARLYLE

Home

The largest part of our happiness is found at home. Here we create a loving environment where we surround ourselves with treasured objects and celebrate quiet, ordinary moments with family and friends. Our home is the only place on earth we have control over. We're free to paint our bathroom ceiling sky blue and turn our rooms into gardens, beaches, woods, and conservatories. Within the privacy of our walls, we're free to create the most joyful environment that enlarges our love of life, cultivates and inspires us to celebrate life in the modest rhythms of the everyday.

The one essential thing is that we strive to have light in ourselves.

ALBERT SCHWEITZER

We come home to our senses. Nowhere can we enjoy lingering conversations at the kitchen table better than in the privacy of our homes. When we putter about, watering the plants, we feel we are cultivating our inner garden. When we iron a blue and yellow floral tablecloth, we look forward to the evening meal as well as recall the day we found the cloth in Provence. As we anticipate a child's walking through the door, we feel the tenderness of love, the sweetness of life, and the intimacy of home.

The Mind's internal heaven shall shed her dews of inspiration on the humblest day.

WILLIAM WORDSWORTH

As we move mindfully from room to room, we recollect the symbolic meanings behind the things around us. Peter and I continuously try to "love up" our home, make improvements where needed, upgrade and maintain it the best we can. As much as we love our privacy, we also relish having friends come into our intimate haven. We carry

They know enough who know how to learn.

HENRY ADAMS

the sacredness of home within our bosom wherever we go. Home is the ground of our being.

your ten words

I have often invited my audiences to write down their ten defining words. What began as a fun exercise eventually led to a huge body of research. I now have collected thousands of examples. By staying mindful of what we love, of what we cherish and hold dear, we can cultivate our words in tangible ways, watering the seeds of our consciousness with every step we take, every thought we have, in all the wonderfully creative ways we express our love of life.

I urge you to write down your ten defining words. It's a happy exercise that is extremely revealing. I've shown you mine. Now it is your turn to write down yours. Light a candle, sit in a favorite spot, and let your intuition identify "Who am I?"

twenty-five words

Another fun exercise to further expand your awareness is to write down twenty-five words for each one of your ten words. For example, take one of my words—*home*. What comes to mind? Write twenty-five words as fast as you can. Let them flow out of you. What associations do you have with *home*? My associations are *love, hearth, private, cheerful, pretty, friends, intimate, flowers, happy, children, tenderness, sweet, sacred, grounded, sensuous, welcoming, color–*

ful, beautiful, comfortable, family, light, friendly, art, collections, changing.

When we focus on what we love, we fashion our life around our inner knowledge. We live the life we choose, surrounding ourselves with people we love and objects that hold great meaning. Home is a good place to begin our concentration because it is our emotional center. Then we can branch out in all directions, spreading the light of our true essence and heart's desire.

There's only one corner of the universe you can be certain of improving and that's your own self.

ALDOUS HUXLEY

creating our values

We are creative beings. Each of us is creative and productive in imaginative and original ways. By what we do, we contribute to life from our unique inner knowledge. I know a lot of people who don't think of themselves as being particularly creative. They're more analytical, more mathematical, more logical. Nonetheless, we're all creative. The act of creating covers a vast number of activities and attitudes, and it is something accessible to all of us.

People should be beautiful in every way . . . in their thoughts and in their innermost selves.

ANTON CHEKHOV

Keep in mind that when we choose happiness now, we do so not only to create tangible things—raise a family, design buildings or gardens or create paintings. Happiness is about creating healthy emotions: goodness, kindness, love, loyalty, truth, beauty, and unity.

affirming life

I suggest you study certain philosophers who have a positive outlook on life. I have dozens of notebooks filled with affirmations, quotations, and notes about thoughts and ways to choose a healthier, more satisfying, and happier life. This course of study over a lifetime is a concrete tool to guide us into greater concentration on what is light-filled, beautiful, and loving.

All growth—psychological, moral, spiritual—calls for continual beginning.

MARY PATRICIA SEXTON

Our consciousness wants our positive participation. Each day we can say an affirmation about ourselves: "I am a kind, caring person." "I am a lover of beauty." "I am a loyal person." "I am a seeker of truth." "I am a good person." By saying yes to your true nature, you will be making a strong connection to your highest values.

precious keys to finding happiness

At the end of this book I list keys to finding true happiness. In the process of answering the question "Who am I?," we stay in touch with our self-mastery, our ability to control ourselves in such a way that our thoughts, words, and actions are authentic reflections of our happier self. We pay attention to our own light through self-awareness, self-discovery, self-evaluation, self-exploration, self-expression, self-acceptance, and self-love.

answering the questions

Here, I'm going to pose these fifty-four precious keys as questions that will help keep us focused on defining "Who am I?"
These questions can be answered yes or no, but many could be
scored from 1 to 10, with 1 representing a low
degree and 10 representing a high degree.
You decide what makes you feel most comfortable. I answered them yes or no the first
time I read them and then I wrote down a
score for selected questions. For example,
"Are you doing everything with enthusiasm?"
This question would be most useful if it were honestly answered
by the score method. I have not numbered the keys because they
are all vitally important. Together they work as tools to help us
identify, evaluate and answer "Who am I?" Keep them in your
heart as you proceed on your path toward choosing greater,
lasting happiness.

*Our responsible
concern is with our
private destiny, after
all.*

WILLIAM JAMES

As part of your mindfulness practice, read over these questions once a week and write down your answers. Compare your
responses with those from previous weeks. Are
you moving in the direction of your goal to
know yourself better and to be true to your
heart? These questions and your answers will
unlock the door, shedding light on the happiness potential that is already inside you waiting to be born and reborn with each new
sunrise.

*If you begin to
understand what you
are without trying to
change it, then what
you are undergoes a
transformation.*

KRISHNAMURTI

❀ Are you finding and pursuing your passion?

❀ Are you concentrating on and nurturing your mind with your best thoughts and with good literature?

❀ Are you recognizing and honoring your own higher, happier self and your inner spirit?

❀ Are you always trying to express your unique creative spirit?

❀ Are you growing in a deeper commitment to your life and the life around you?

❀ Are you creating and surrounding yourself with beauty?

❀ Are you living each moment now?

❀ Are you doing everything with enthusiasm?

❀ Are your ideas lighting up the world for you?

❀ Do you trust your intuition as your inner intelligence?

❀ Are you letting your imagination blossom?

❀ Are you living in gratitude for the gift of your life and in appreciation of the lives of loved ones?

❀ Are you cultivating self-knowledge and free will?

❀ Are you making keen use of your five senses, becoming a sensualist?

❀ Are you celebrating life fully with laughter and fun?

❀ Are you keeping the child within you alive?

❀ Are you regularly communing with and learning from nature?

❀ Are you stimulating your curiosity and sense of wonder?

❀ Do you recognize that flowers create paradise on earth?

❀ Do you let color celebrate your world with joy?

❀ Do you allow music to transport you?

❀ Do you believe your sense of humor reflects your sense of proportion?

❈ Do you believe perseverance is the
  essential ingredient for all personal
  achievements?

❈ Do you practice and express kindness?

❈ When it rains, do you look for the
  rainbow?

❈ Are you maintaining loyalty?

❈ Are you vigorously confronting challenges through
  inner strength and courage?

❈ Throughout the changing circumstances of life, are you
  seeking and maintaining balance and simplicity?

❈ Do you believe that order precedes beauty and struc-
  tures all things?

❈ Are you making wise and careful choices?

❈ Are you developing your spirit-energy in regular times
  of contemplation?

❈ Are you a constant student of truth?

❈ Are you growing in generosity and clarity?

❈ Do you believe tolerance is a virtue?

❈ Are you learning to forgive?

❈ Are you cultivating deep understanding?

❈ Do you believe freedom makes civilization possible?

❈ Are you growing in humility?

❈ Do you believe a sense of timing is crucial?

❈ Do you believe integrity and character define you?

❈ Are you open to changing circumstances, while remaining flexible?

❈ Do you exercise common sense?

*Everything is perfect
but there is a lot of
room for
improvement.*

SHUNRYN SUZUKI

*Make your life
something beautiful
for God.*

MOTHER TERESA

- Are you establishing and maintaining healthy living habits through self-discipline?
- Are you patient with yourself and with others?
- Do you accept what you cannot change?
- Are you nonjudgmental?
- Are you sustaining hope and faith?
- Do you believe caring is an act of grace?
- Do you extend compassion and empathy everywhere to everyone?
- Do you find ways to serve others?
- Do you live each day by the Golden Rule?
- Do you communicate unconditional love?

CHAPTER 3

give energy, get energy

Success is dependent on effort.
—SOPHOCLES

Action may not always bring happiness;
but there is no happiness without action.
—BENJAMIN DISRAELI

the dramatic gift of enthusiasm

Ralph Waldo Emerson wrote the famous line: "Nothing great was ever achieved without enthusiasm." Enthusiasm is a gift because it implies excitement and interest. So many people sleepwalk through life, mindlessly doing mundane things without being enthusiastic. Children are enthusiastic while many adults tend to get bogged down and lose the vital energy of

*Energy is the power
that drives every
human being. It is not
lost by exertion but
maintained by it.*

GERMAINE GREER

enthusiasm. When we passionately pay attention to what interests us, we can be enthusiastic about hundreds of different things in our
life, from dancing to eating a delicious meal,
to water-skiing, singing, or teaching.

We can teach ourselves how to live exuber-
antly now, right in the heart of this moment.
When we nourish each fresh experience, we
have all our juices flowing and there is never a dull moment.

Whatever you are excited about will increase your vitality.
Enthusiastic people tend to be optimists and avoid becoming
cynical. Together we should try to let our love of life shine
through everything we think, all our ideas, our words, and our
actions. The word *enthusiasm* is from the Greek *enthousiasmos,*
rooted in *entheos,* meaning inspired, or having the god within.

A young friend recently remarried a man she is hopelessly
in love with but who travels a great deal for his real estate business. When he is away, she told me, she is seriously unhappy.
She asked me to advise her on how to become happier when
Donald is away. We sat in her garden sipping iced tea as I listened. She told me all the things that make her happy. She loves
to ride horses, loves to go camping, adores the beach, and loves

*You are in charge of
what enters your
mind.*

SUE PATTON THOELE

to go to art galleries. Laura told me she is
wildly excited browsing in discount stores such
as Target, Wal-Mart, Kmart and Home Depot,
where she finds useful things for the children,
the house, and the garden. Donald was in
Australia when we had our afternoon visit
together, and Laura seemed as happy as could be. She smiled
and told me Donald would be home in two days. She said with

a giggle, "I think I'm going to pack up the kids and we'll take off for the beach for two days and arrive home just before Donald walks through the door. This will be fun." When she consciously thought about it, Laura knew what made her happy, and she acted on her knowl- *Simply being alive is* edge and went to the beach. The two days of *the greatest blessing* swimming and playing with the children in *we can enjoy.* the sand made Laura enthusiastic to go home,
set a pretty table, cook a favorite dinner, and

RENÉ DUBOS

exude positive, happy energy toward Donald upon his arrival. The inner spark is infectious.

The way to increase our energy is to find lots and lots of things to be enthusiastic about. Whether it is a clean house, a freshly stocked refrigerator, or a newly mowed lawn, there are opportunities everywhere for us to become excited and thoroughly enjoy what we choose to do. Recently, Peter and I had lunch with dear friends we see all too infrequently because Toby lives in San Francisco and Fran lives in Chicago. There was laughter and tears of joy; we all told sentimental stories, and the energy was exhilarating. We were happy to be together and were charged up, feeling uplifted and grateful for having had the visit. We shared books we were reading, caught up on trips taken and things we were doing that were
stimulating and fun. Fran had stars in her *Life is ours to spend,* eyes, as she was soon to head to Paris on a *not to be saved.* business trip.

D. H. LAWRENCE

Try not to waste precious energy complaining. It is far better to face what is bothering us and to do something about it than to dwell on something negative that dampens our spirits and the spirits of those around us. As parents, the

Action is eloquence.

SHAKESPEARE

greatest treasure we can give our children and grandchildren is to raise them in a happy environment, where they learn from their family just how joyful life can be. Through discipline and determination, we teach ourselves to remain present to the potential enthusiasm in each moment. We increase our capacity by creating fun, stimulating times in the midst of our ordinary lives. An enthusiastic outlook on life makes every moment an adventure. Life is to be celebrated, not merely lived. Today is the time; here, where we are, is the place.

The world is so full of a number of things, I'm sure we should all be as happy as kings.

ROBERT LOUIS

STEVENSON

Enthusiasm is an internal emotional state. Give each moment your undivided attention, and you will feel the intense excitement of being alive. Refuse to take this miracle of the gift of life for granted. The world owes us nothing. We're here to play our part, and if Emerson was right that nothing great was ever achieved without enthusiasm, then our life, moment to moment, should be a tribute to the potential to make small moments great and link them together, one after another, throughout all our days and nights.

being around positive energy

We get good vibes by giving them. Being around people who exude positive energy is stimulating and inspiring. They're fun to be with because they have the power to uplift our spirits as they uplift their own. They invite us to actively participate in the infinite possibilities for living more radiantly. Someone with a good disposition, who is cheerful and looks on the bright side of life, generates lots of good energy. For example, I buy my groceries at a Korean-owned market because I always enjoy the experience. The people there know my name, smile at me, and genuinely want to be helpful. The conversation is simple but caring: "How are you today, Alexandra? You selected nice fresh tulips. I love yellow tulips, too. You look nice today in your red jacket. How is Mr. Brown? How are the girls? I picked a nice ripe cantaloupe for you. Have a great evening. See you tomorrow." When we show genuine appreciation to others for what they do for us, we share and increase each other's positive energy.

> *Ecstasy is a full, deep involvement in life.*
>
> JOHN LOWELL

There is a tiny restaurant near our apartment in New York where we go regularly. We started going there just after it opened and always have such a good time. We are greeted with "Come right in." We are thanked upon leaving with "Thank you for coming." The chef comes out to shake our hands. "I made the spinach just for you." Everyone is upbeat. Everyone feels good. The atmosphere is one of caring, love, and kindness, a place where we feel a welcome part of the family.

A smile, good eye contact, a pat on the shoulder, an inquiry about someone's new apartment, asking how the applications are coming along for a teaching position, trying to remember the new busboy's name, being fully present, listening well—these small gestures of caring are magical when they become a habit, a happy continuing experience. An inquiry about someone's day, asking questions

> *It is astonishing how short a time it takes for very wonderful things to happen.*
>
> FRANCES HODGSON
> BURNETT

Genius is mainly an affair of energy.

MATTHEW ARNOLD

about their interests, remembering to ask about a movie a friend saw or to ask how a dinner party turned out sweetens life. Spreading positive energy toward others is always the appropriate thing to do. When we sincerely care about others, it is easy to think of things that will uplift them. When we affirm and confirm our own life, as well as the lives of the people we're in contact with regularly, the atmosphere is one of progress and acceptance. Good feelings are great energy boosters.

your physical energy

We're meant to live active lives in order to keep our energy up. Whenever we move our feet we become more energetic. On a scale from 1 to 10, what is your general energy level? Do you consider yourself a lively person, someone who is active, full of energy most of the time? What are some activities you do to exert your energy? How active are you day to day? Do you do housecleaning? Do you exercise by doing stretches once a day? Do you work out at a gym or health club? Do you lift weights? Do you swim for exercise? Do you jog or ride a bicycle? How often do you go for walks? How long are they? Do you do yoga? Do you dance for exercise? Do you horseback ride? Do you do

Live with no time out.

SIMONE DE BEAUVOIR

tai chi? Do you ski? Do you play tennis or basketball? Do you enjoy hiking or mountain climbing? Do you play golf? Do you have Swedish massages regularly to increase your energy? Do you have reflexology treatments for your feet to redirect your energy throughout your body?

We release energy by doing activities we enjoy. For example, no matter how comfortable we feel in bed in the morning, when we're in the habit of getting up early and going for a vigorous walk or jog for twenty minutes, we look forward to this activity as a pleasant way to begin each day.

Was it done with enjoyment?

JOHN RUSKIN

I know many people who have no formal exercise regime but who are extremely active and vigorous. Young mothers who run after small children and take care of the house, and who also manage to fit in some tennis or swimming, don't necessarily have to take aerobics classes to stay fit. They can ride a bicycle with a child, walk the dog, and, when they're really fortunate, go dancing from time to time with their husbands.

jumping, climbing, romping

Our positive energy shines through activities we enjoy. If we love what we're doing, we can jump for joy—literally. A friend couldn't find any exercise that she enjoyed, but she remembered jumping and tumbling on a trampoline as a child. She discovered she could exercise on a "rebounder," doing aerobics that use gravity to cleanse her energy system, maximize her vitality, and (she feels) add years to her life. Jumping on her round rebounder (a miniature trampoline) got me excited. I acquired one and am enjoying it enormously. A few minutes a day gets me energized. I feel invigorated, childlike, and playful.

Live your life while you have it. Life is a splendid gift.

FLORENCE

NIGHTINGALE

Climbing stairs is also a great energy booster for me. When

we're at the cottage, I run upstairs as often as I can. It only takes a moment and it stirs my blood. I love the feeling of releasing my energy, letting it freely flow, and I become transformed. Whether climbing steps, stairs, or mountains, climbing is good for our heart, lungs and vitality.

We have no more right to consume happiness without producing it than to consume wealth without producing it.

GEORGE BERNARD SHAW

One of my favorite energy releases is going for a romp with our daughter and son-in-law's golden retriever, Carter. When he walks, I walk. When he trots, I trot. And when he canters, I fly through the air with him as though I were a teenager. I especially love romping on the beach when the waves are high. Whether you run in a park, fly a kite, walk hand in hand under the stars with a spouse or lover, go on a scooter or play ball, put your energy out there and you will feel more vitally alive.

energy flashes

When we are sensitive to our feelings, moment to moment, being alert to what we are experiencing, we will have energy flashes or surges that give us a feeling of relief, pleasure, and joy. Knowing and understanding our energy is key to freeing up great resources of positive feelings. We can train ourselves to be aware of our energy as it moves throughout our body.

I've taken my fun where I've found it.

RUDYARD KIPLING

I suffered severe whiplash after battling to survive in the aftermath of Hurricane Bonnie for thirty-eight minutes in rough waves off Watch Hill, Rhode Island. To heal,

I had finger pressure massage treatments, using a Japanese technique called shiatsu. These massages were therapeutic and relaxing as well as being invigorating. There are fourteen meridians or energy pathways in the body, and the goal of this kind of healing is to regain balance by unblocking energy trapped in these meridians. What I found fascinating was that the more Anna worked with finger pressure on my neck, the more I felt energy flashing through my entire body, down to the tips of my toes. Energy flow and transformation feels revitalizing and invigorates us.

Great peace is found in little busy-ness.

GEOFFREY CHAUCER

not by touch

Be tuned in to your natural energy surges, not only those brought on by touch. Pay attention to the flashes. Once I told clients that they shouldn't live with anything that they didn't love in their new apartment. I explained that when you find items that give you goosebumps and a tingling sensation throughout your body, and make your face flush, you'll know those are the ones to buy if you can. These clients didn't feel the goosebumps and didn't buy anything for a year! They weren't ready; they were just beginning to experience what was out there, to take stock, take measurements, and take their time. After a year, things began to click. They felt energized and got goosebumps. "We love this table." "We love this fabric." "That's it." "Look no further." "I love this painting." They needed to feel comfortable with what they were

Do things to make your day precious.

BERNIE SIEGEL

The little known act of being happy.

VOLTAIRE

doing. When they began, it was all business. They were not in touch with the emotional side of decorating, only the serious financial side—the things that must be done, the choices that must be made. We talked budgets. The thought of becoming vulnerable, being open to serendipity, to falling in love with objects and then working them into the scheme seemed to them a foreign way to think and act. But time healed the divisions between their rational brain and the body's energy surges and opened the way for them to follow their hearts.

Look for the energy flashes and feel the surges in moments where everything comes together beautifully. When all the right elements are in place, there is a feeling we get, a tingling, a release of energy, a sense of flow and transformation that informs us that we are here, we are home, this is it. Look no further.

movement is all

Whether we are graceful, awkward, romantic, or pedestrian, if we give energy, we will get energy as though supplied with an electric current. There is nothing better to boost our spirits than to get going, to move about. We should be mindful of our energy boosts when we do what has to be done. As we move our feet, breathing deeply, we expand our awareness of what it means to be alive. I have a client who paces up and down his apartment with a clipboard, thinking through solutions to problems. Our bodies were designed to be vigorous. I remember when I had a bad back and couldn't move freely

Enthusiasm is the invisible inward intensity of being.

EPRE

for several months. For someone as physically active as I am, this was an extremely difficult adjustment. I had to accept the reality that my back would heal naturally but that it would take time. As a compromise I had a brace made so that I could sit up for short periods of time and do a little walking.

When we pay attention to movement, we realize there are hundreds of little errands we can run, moving from room to room, to keep our minds more alert as we keep our body more agile. Sitting in one position for long periods of time without moving is bad for our circulation and can even be dangerous to our health. Rather than trying to save steps, try different ways to create more movement in your daily routine.

When a man dies, if he can pass enthusiasm along to his children, he has left them an estate of incalculable value.

THOMAS EDISON

The American dancer and choreographer Martha Graham, a central figure in modern dance, lived ninety-seven years. Her secret was movement. "There is a vitality, a life force, an energy, a quickening," she taught us, "that is translated through you into action, and because there is only one of you in all time, this expression is unique. And if you block it, it will never exist through any other medium and will be lost."

Dare to be naïve.

BUCKMINSTER FULLER

energy boosts

Here are some simple, practical suggestions on how to add more movement to boost your spirits, create more energy, and have more fun.

❀ Go for a fifteen-minute fast walk every morning as soon as you wake up. If the weather is bad, do your routine inside. Put on your sweats and sneakers and move from your kitchen through the hall and into the living room, the bedroom and back again. Set a kitchen timer to go off when your time is up.

❀ If possible, walk to work or from the train or bus station or leave your car parked in a space several blocks from your office. Arriving with pink cheeks and your lungs full of fresh air sets the tone for your day.

❀ When seated at your desk at home, if you have the instinct to stretch, stand up and do some simple arm stretches. While you're up, go to the powder room, wash your hands, put on some hand cream and cologne and walk back to your workplace refreshed. This will not distract you from your concentration but will encourage you and help you focus with more clarity.

❀ Our wonderful holistic doctor urges Peter and me to carry home our groceries, not have them delivered. If you live miles away from the store, drive, but don't seek help from a child or spouse unpacking the car. Dr. McLean also encourages us to carry our own suitcases at train stations or airports, rather than calling a porter. Lift the bags up and down to strengthen your arms as though you were lifting weights.

❀ When you feel intense and need to release some excess energy, vacuum the floors, the rugs, or even the upholstered furniture. Ten minutes of cleaning stirs your juices and makes you feel revitalized. If you don't like vacuuming, paint the picket fence, mow the lawn, rake the leaves, or build a bookcase.

❀ After writing a letter or paying a bill, walk to the post office or mailbox to mail it and feel the instant satisfaction of having achieved something constructive.

❀ Turn your mattress every other week. Doing so makes you sleep better, and you'll feel you are turning over a new leaf for joyful rest.

❀ Buy rubber knee pads and scrub your bathroom floor. You will be gratified with the sparkling result.

❀ Play some favorite music when you're alone in the house, so you can groove to the rhythms as you tidy from room to room.

❀ The next time you consider hiring a painter to repaint a room, have a serious conversation with your spouse and see if you can agree to do it together instead. You'll save money and have good conversations, and if you each use two paint brushes, you'll be ambidextrous and strengthen your arms and back.

❀ Find a television exercise show and bend and stretch with it or buy some tapes to use when convenient.

❀ If you live in a city, explore the more attractive streets for walking where you may need to go. Build in extra time to walk part of the way to appointments, even if you take a bus or taxi the rest of the way.

You can't cross the sea merely by staring at the water.

RABINDRANATH

TAGORE

People seldom see the halting and painful steps by which the most insignificant success is achieved.

ANNIE SULLIVAN

- If you live in the country and have fallen trees on your property, chop your own firewood.
- The reasons to have a garden are to experience the awesome beauty of nature and also to be digging in the soil, getting sweaty, dirty, and earthy. Use both hands to work in order to balance your body's energy.
- The next time you are at the beach, build a sandcastle. The wet sand weighs a lot and you will be invigorated by your creation.
- Toss a ball, catch a ball, and have fun.
- When you're really over-the-top happy, skip. There's something quite magical about skipping.
- Buy a jump rope. Jumping rope improves our balance and builds strength.
- If you've been sitting at a desk for several hours, jump up and down or march in place for thirty to fifty repetitions, bringing your knees up as high as you can. Swing your arms back and forth. Smile. Pleasurable feelings follow.

don't get stuck—do something

Think of using your energy to help others as well as yourself. There are many quick, exciting ways to do this. Whether we give

I believe we learn by practice.

MARTHA GRAHAM

a gift to a friend, a compliment to a stranger, or a donation to a favorite charity, whatever positive vibrations we send out come back to us in rich benefits. We become more alive the more we give of ourselves. Life requires us to use our power by spreading our energy far and wide as well as in focused ways.

The more often we give off good energy—even if only in optimistic, compassionate thoughts and insightful ideas—the more opportunities we'll have to live vibrantly moment to moment.

To live a happier life, we must appreciate every detail of the present experience, because nothing will ever happen exactly the same way again. Appreciation energizes. The spur-of-the-moment get-together, the spontaneous urge to call a friend, these energy flashes inform us that we may need to sit down at our desk and write a soulful letter to a friend, or we may need to visit a friend in the hospital or drop in on a friend who is alone, elderly, and lonely. Do it now, because this is the only time you can be sure to make a difference. Listen and respond. Pay attention to timing. You will feel exhilarated when you obey these energy signals. They are inner choices longing to be heard. You'll never know how much a simple, quick gesture can mean to someone else.

When we try to live in touch with our deepest desires and yearnings, we're sometimes able to fling out our energy. Other times, we're challenged to focus on our own immediate needs and desires. We wisely extend our energy as we harness it in a rhythmic pattern to fit the circumstances of our immediate lives.

Many people love us and rely on us in varied ways. A large degree of our happiness is our relationships to others. It's nice to be needed, to feel that others care about us, that we are making a positive difference in their lives. Because it is our responsibility and commitment to keep our energy up, we have to be

Don't judge each day by the harvest you reap but by the seeds you plant.

ROBERT LOUIS
STEVENSON

To love what you do and feel that it matters—how could anything be more fun?

KATHERINE GRAHAM

determined not to get stuck. There is always something we can do—right now—to increase our good energy.

Creating is easy if you view the world as if you were a child. Playing and creating are almost synonymous.

BERNIE SIEGEL

I get a great deal of energy from loving life, from my work, from all the wonderful people I spend time with day to day. But if Peter or I get sick or one of our children is in pain or trouble and needs me, or there is a traumatic event that requires complete attention, I focus my energy more specifically. We cannot give out more energy than we have. There are times when we want to be calm, more self-contained; to be alone for a while, using our energy for self-healing.

Whether we feel the need to rearrange our clothes closets and weed out the garments that no longer fit or that we no longer adore, or we want to spend more time reading, we will feel energized when we're mindful of our own needs. If I feel tired and need a break, I'll cut back on other commitments for a while to give myself some buffer time. If I'm trying to meet a deadline, I'll say no to any outside distractions or detours.

The more I do, the more I can do.

CHRISTOPHER REEVE

When we decide what we want to do with our life, and move in the direction of our goals, when we challenge ourselves to personal growth as a regular discipline, we put everything we have into everything we do. This is what invigorates us.

What are some of the things that exhaust you? It could simply be humidity. Or perhaps people who chronically complain sap you of your energy. Often, lack of exercise drains our vitality. Overeating also tends to make us feel sluggish. To know happiness personally, it is just as important to know what depletes us as what stimulates us.

nap or groove?

If I am merely tired, I may decide to lie down on the living room sofa and read a book until I fall asleep. Or I may need some fresh air. I may choose to take a gathering basket to the market and enjoy selecting fruit—grapefruit, blueberries, green grapes, cherries, apples, and clementines—anticipating a relaxed, colorful, and delicious breakfast the next morning. Or, perhaps I feel I need an appointment at the hair salon, a private time off from any obligations or demands. There is nothing quite like a haircut and styling to elevate my spirits. The outer improvement definitely lifts us up.

> *We are a society that finds it difficult to discover the exuberant joy and spontaneity of childhood.*
>
> SIR THOMAS MOORE

I always try to figure out what's not working and do something about it as quickly as possible. When some stockings I'd ordered arrived by mail in the wrong color, my immediate reaction was disappointment. Then I switched gears; I decided to make it work out. I called the hosiery shop. They apologized for the error and said that they had the color I ordered in stock and on sale. I went on a fifty-block pilgrimage to exchange the kelly-green pair of stockings for the chartreuse shade I'd ordered. I window-shopped down to the store and back, and stopped in the home stretch for a decaf espresso. I picked up a pound of fresh coffee beans to grind for breakfast. I returned home refreshed, full of

> *Happiness does not lie in results, but in the effort.*
>
> DOSTOYEVSKY

vitality and enthusiasm. I had a wonderful outing—what in our family we call a groove.

When something gives us pleasure, it is never a waste of time. It wasn't just the chartreuse stockings I picked up at half price that boosted my happiness. It was the fun of the entire experience. I used the mishap as an opportunity to go on a groove, giving myself time to clear my head. My legs were happy to have the exercise; my lungs were full of sunshine. I felt ready to tackle the world.

the carrot theory: the fun of anticipation

Ever since I received my first paycheck from an interior design firm years ago, I've always wanted to go out to dinner on Friday nights to celebrate. I know many couples think restaurants are too expensive and don't want to waste their time and money, but I love restaurants. Over the years I've enjoyed developing the carrot theory. No matter what I have to endure, I plan for some little indulgence at the end, some sensuous delight or a pampering ritual that I can enjoy both anticipating and experiencing.

> *I make the most of all that comes and the least of all that goes.*
>
> SARA TEASDALE

Living well means putting a big emphasis on having some fun. When I was a little girl, I loved having a baby-sitter play with us on the nights my parents went out. It always made me happy when my parents were having a good time. Why should we ever outgrow our capacity for having fun? If you prefer staying home on Friday nights after a long week at the office or traveling, having a romantic candlelit home-cooked dinner is the carrot you may anticipate and appreciate. If we are home all week, however, getting out of the house may be the carrot.

I used to have an older friend who finished every evening meal with one scoop of chocolate ice cream and one piece of Godiva milk chocolate— never two, but one of each. This was her carrot. We are the one who chooses what carrots we wish to have in our life. The carrot theory is not about overindulgence; rather, it creates stimulation and balance. If we practice living mindfully day by day, these carrots of anticipation can be the rendezvous of pleasure celebrating our life being lived well.

The most wasted day of all is that on which we have not laughed.

SÉBASTIEN CHAMFORT

Living by the carrot theory increases our momentary happiness. Do your best in each situation and then reward yourself. I remember going to a New York hospital to have minor surgery. I wore a blue dress that I felt good in and I had a delicious cozy lunch at a favorite neighborhood restaurant with Peter before I was admitted to the hospital. A few days later I left the hospital and we headed straight to an Italian restaurant, where I had some fried shrimp and artichoke hearts—a carrot that I could anticipate while being deprived of fine dining in the hospital.

Often when Peter and I fly home from a vacation trip, we don't eat the airplane food—instead, we drop our bags at home and go directly to a neighborhood restaurant to enjoy a romantic moment together before going home to an empty refrigerator and a huge stack of newspapers and mail. This moment extends the pleasure of our journey, allowing us to ease our way back into the

Most folks are about as happy as they make up their minds to be.

ABRAHAM LINCOLN

rhythms of our domestic and professional lives. We can sit comfortably after a cramped flight, sip a glass of chardonnay, have a bite to eat, and enjoy a good visit together before going home.

There is no wealth but life.

JOHN RUSKIN

The carrot theory, by balancing our lives so that our energy is revitalized, refreshed, and inspired, helps us to keep our perspective. Mini breaks from serving others, when we take tender care of our own desires and emotional needs, keeps our vital energy alive, sustains our well-being, and keeps us living a happier life.

giving and receiving "ninis"

When I traveled around the world in 1959–60 with my aunt, Ruth Elizabeth Johns, we visited thirty-three cities in thirteen countries. My aunt was a pioneering social worker. I knew she had very little money, yet she generously invited her three oldest nieces to go on this three-month trip. As a teenager, totally inexperienced in ways of the world, I was amazed that my aunt could produce little gifts for everyone she saw—friends who greeted her at the airport, people who invited us to stay in their homes. I experienced firsthand how much it meant to her and her friends to give and receive love through the little gifts they exchanged.

All that we need to make us really happy is something to be enthusiastic about.

CHARLES KINGSLEY

In many countries that we visited, it was the custom to give a gift to a guest who enters your home. The memory of these gestures magnifies as I grow more mature. I received lacquer bowls, chopsticks, spoons, candles, handkerchiefs, and notecards. The law of karma was demonstrated brilliantly as we gave gifts and were given presents in equal proportion. This act of kindness as a custom has left a deep impression on me. Over the years it has led our family to the ritual of exchanging "ninis," a form of generous, happy reciprocity.

When my daughters were young they were insatiable for gifts, a passion that increased over the years. I always brought them gifts when I came home from a trip, even if I was only away one night. The presents were usually small and inexpensive, often bought at an airport gift shop or a hotel. Over the years we called these little nothings "ninis."

The more you lose yourself in something bigger than yourself, the more energy you will have.

NORMAN VINCENT
PEALE

I can't imagine life without these small gifts that let others know that we love them and are thinking of them when we are not together. A nini is something that costs next to nothing. It could be a small square of chocolate served with your espresso at a restaurant, or a fresh bar of soap from the hotel room. Sometimes we gift wrap the ninis, other times we put them in small, pretty shopping bags with colorful tissue paper. If the spirit moves us, we can put a nini in a small box wrapped in perky paper and tied with ribbon. There are no rules to ninis other than the joy of the giver in connecting with the receiver.

Some of my favorite ninis from family and friends are several packages of Day-Glo ribbons in chartreuse, fuschia, purple, and orange; a pot of primroses; blue mitts to replace a stained old potholder; a bar of lily-of-the-valley soap for the bath; miniature nail clippers you can't leave home without;

colorful cocktail napkins; a personal photograph in a pretty frame; some blue-and-white checked tissue paper; some note-cards in a pretty box; a bar of lilac soap; a clear glass bud vase; a pair of hand-painted geranium hand towels; a chartreuse-and-clear-striped toothbrush; a Zen poetry book; some colorful pastel file folders purchased by my daughter on a business trip to Paris; matches from a shared favorite restaurant; colorful elastic bands in fuchsia, chartreuse, orange, and apple green; and pocket notebooks in purple, yellow, pink, and green.

Success is a twinkle in the eye, a generosity of spirit, a palpable energy projected from a loving heart, and a caring soul.

VAL J. HALAMANDARIS

Other ninis are miniature colored pencils to travel with; a chartreuse round paper box for paper clips; a bottle of Levenger's "Pinkly" ink; a piece of crystal bought at an airport in Colorado; a sheet of *Love* postal stamps; a scented candle; a jasmine sachet for my drawer; a few yards of French ribbon; a package of flowered wrapping paper; a selection of Nile-blue paper and envelopes; a coffee mug attractively designed; some nail protein for a split nail; ink cartridges from France in a tin box; a fuchsia-and-white-checked zippered jewelry travel bag; a funky pair of red and black stockings; a purple leather belt purchased from a street vendor; a cotton handkerchief in fuchsia and acid green to wear as a bandana; sticks of red and blue sealing wax, some bath gel from Crabtree & Evelyn; a clip for my hair; a red mechanical pencil; a CD of Charlotte Church's "Voice Like an Angel"; some pastel erasers in pink, yellow, blue, peach, and green; and a small music box from a favorite stationery store that plays "As Time Goes By."

thank you

I was raised by a strict mother to write thank you letters. What started as a habit of obligation to write the bread-and-butter letter turned into a passion to reach out to say thank you. We thank someone for the gift they have given, whether tangible or intangible. This healthy habit of expressing thanks shouldn't be limited to a letter, but when we do receive a sweet note from someone who appreciates something we've done for them or something we've given them, it makes us feel wonderful. The ability to freely say and write thank you is a sign of good energy and well-being.

Let us be grateful to people who make us happy; they are the charming gardeners who make our souls blossom.

MARCEL PROUST

We have an abundance of people we should and could thank for the rich blessings of our lives. No one is self-made. We are all thrown together in the present moment doing a variety of things, trying to make our way, trying to make a difference. The tiny acts of kindness we're given each day are cumulative in volume and significance. Expressing thanks from a full heart raises our consciousness of the goodness in the world.

A florist called me recently to inquire if I had received a bouquet of flowers sent by friends in Georgia. I indeed had and I'd never seen such a beautiful basket full of red and pink roses with giant pink peonies and lemon leaves. I went into rhapsodic verse about the joy this surprise bouquet brought me as well as everyone who walked through our front door. Apparently, the giver of the flowers had not received my letter of thanks, so I wrote a second thank you to our friends as well as one to the people who created the arrangement. The flower shop was glad to receive my thanks for the most memorable and extraordinary bouquet.

Walter, a chef friend in Connecticut who orders organic tomatoes for me, pinned on the wall of his restaurant a picture I took of the tomatoes on a blue-and-white-striped tablecloth and sent along with a thank you note. Most people write thank you notes for a tangible object—flowers, a box of stationery, or perhaps a book. Many of our notes begin "Thank you for the . . ." On a scale of 1 to 10, how do you rate yourself on writing your thank you notes? Do you enjoy it or is it a chore you sometimes dread? Certainly, saying thank you is more enjoyable when you sit at a writing table or desk where you have notepaper you adore, your up-to-date address book, and stamps near at hand, as well as a favorite fountain pen.

> *Man needs for his happiness, not only the enjoyment of this or that, but hope and enterprise and change.*
>
> BERTRAND RUSSELL

Years ago, I got in the habit of writing thank you notes to Ellen, the woman who runs a cleaning service I use in New York. We've never met, although we talk on the telephone and I write her a note each time I pay a bill. Once she gave me a box of Japanese sweets as a gift of thanks for my letters. Not long ago a client wanted to know how to clean a lacquer coffee table I'd sold her. When I wrote Ellen to inquire, I received a small shopping bag brimming with magical yellow furniture cleaning rags as a gift to use and share with my client.

As a businesswoman, I receive checks for payment. I'm always grateful and deposit them into the bank account, but the ones accompanied by a nice note from a happy client mean the world to me. I save each note, glad to have found it sprinkled among all the impersonal paperwork. Thanking people for services they perform for you can bring dignity and pleasure to their jobs. The extra little effort, whether made in person, over the telephone, or in writing, adds grace to the giver as well as the receiver and encourages the energy of happiness. When we don't convey our thanks, we often hurt another's feelings. A friend goes to a tremendous amount of trouble to find the right birthday gift. The dry cleaner is conscientious enough to remove a stain from a garment or to re-line a favorite blazer. We are as appreciative of our friend's thoughtfulness as we are for services rendered to us. Both should be acknowledged with thanks.

Enjoyment is not a goal, it is a feeling that accompanies important ongoing activity.

PAUL GOODMAN

It is important for grown children to thank their parents for a weekend visit or for dinner at a wonderful restaurant. Knowing everyone had a good time isn't enough. Expressing thanks in writing relives the happy memory for both the sender and the receiver of the thank you. These admiring notes are uplifting and are an affirmation that things are okay. Being appreciated always increases positive energy, by making us more confident, more certain that life is good.

Someone you love could be going through an emotionally challenging time. Receiving a letter from you thanking them for the friendship, or being able to reread such a letter, may sweeten their dark moment and bring some relief from their loneliness or sense of loss. Genuine appreciation is comforting however you choose to express it.

Thank the bank teller, the bus driver, the clerk at the post office, the salesperson at the office supply store, and the checkout person at the grocery store. The simple act of saying thanks is always appreciated and raises our mutual levels of happiness.

One of my favorite shops in New York has a variety of wonderful items for the home. I love the people who work there, and my clients enjoy going with me when there is a new shipment from Europe to see what treasures have arrived. On one occasion, when I was there on my own, I told a salesperson how gorgeous the sea-foam-green lacquer coffee table with the scallop apron looked in my client's living room in Connecticut. I'd just returned from Darien after seeing the table in place for the first time. "Alexandra, that is so nice to hear," the salesperson replied. "It is really music to my ears. You have no idea how seldom we hear that a client is really happy; we mostly hear complaints. Thank you."

Nothing is virtuous if it is not spontaneous.

MARILYN WILHELM

Many people are quick to find fault but less quick to see good and express thanks. It is a sin of consciousness, an ignorance of mind not to thank someone when they've done something good for us. We should be mindful of reciprocity when we share a cooperative interchange, when we give and take mutually. Think now of all the people to whom you'd like to express thanks.

doing correspondence

In the era of Edith Wharton—before computers took over desk surfaces—there was a ritual of sitting at one's desk doing corre-

spondence. I have a friend who loves to continue this tradition by writing letters of gratitude regularly. Barbara even thanks her family
and friends for *their* thank you notes to her.

I adore pretty stationery, lined envelopes,
and hand-bordered paper. I indulge in fine
notecards and paper because I know I will be
sending them out to sail like a ship. Sharing
them with friends I want to stay connected to,
people I'm grateful to for all they've given to
me and continue to give, is where happiness is.

It is essential to learn to enjoy life. It really does not make sense to go through the motions of existence if one does not appreciate as much of it as possible.

MIHALY

CSIKSZENTMIHALYI

"i'm sorry"

It takes self-confidence to say "I'm sorry." There's something
wonderfully refreshing about admitting it when we're wrong
and doing something about it right away, such as saying "I'm
sorry." We clear our consciences by forgiving ourselves. We all
hurt other people's feelings inadvertently, but most of us try
not to do it deliberately. There are so many different ways that
we can make mistakes. For example:

❂ We forget an appointment.
❂ We are late to a meeting.
❂ We frown.
❂ We don't listen.
❂ We are indiscreet.
❂ We are thoughtless.
❂ We forget a birthday.

- ✹ We are insensitive.
- ✹ We are critical.
- ✹ We are unloving.
- ✹ We are negative.
- ✹ We get shoe polish on the rug.
- ✹ We don't thank someone for a gift.
- ✹ We are unkind or mean.
- ✹ We are angry.
- ✹ We are jealous.
- ✹ We are envious.
- ✹ We are grumpy.
- ✹ We lose our patience.

the footprints

Have there ever been times when you were falsely accused of doing something you hadn't done? When I was ten years old, my mother had roped off the doors to a bedroom after putting shellac on the floor. One of her four children accidentally ran across the still-tacky floor. I was blamed for it. My mother was so angry, screaming out of control. I said, "I'm sorry." This calmed her down but she discovered later that they were not my footprints. She then asked me why I had apologized when I was innocent of wrongdoing. I remember telling her that I didn't feel bad myself, because I hadn't done anything wrong, but I felt sorry for my sister who had done it.

If we do something wrong, our conscience knows and we feel guilty. When we are innocent, we have a clear conscience. Over the years I've been blamed for things, but I try to let the truth guide me. Even when I have done nothing wrong, if someone is upset, I'm glad to say, "I'm sorry," because nothing could be more accurate. I am sorry when people are not happy. So even if you are not guilty of something, say you're sorry, because this actually helps the other person to heal. It is a loving gesture. If someone is critical of our behavior, saying "I'm sorry" helps us to reconnect with the person who is hurting. It also gives us an opportunity to face ourselves, to look more closely at our weaknesses. By being willing to see the situation from another's perspective, we learn how to become more compassionate and loving.

Do what you can,
with what you have,
where you are.

THEODORE ROOSEVELT

The law of cause and effect teaches us that what we put into the world is what we get back. When we are wrong and admit it, we are cleansed. It is a wonderfully refreshing way to clear the air. We are forgiven, we forgive ourselves, and we move on, having grown in understanding.

Most of us try hard to be useful to others, but sometimes we're not available physically or emotionally because of other commitments. There are times when we have to cancel our plans because of an emergency. From my experience, almost everyone will accept our apologies if we are sincere. When we're honest and practice humility, saying we are sorry offers a pathway of relief for the person who feels apologetic. There is a resolution, an understanding, and a uniting where there had been division.

CHAPTER 4

facing the bad stuff

The wise man is he who is contented with
his lot.

—TALMUDIC EXPRESSION

coping well

No matter how we feel or how well we do, we are all marching in
the same direction. How we choose to travel our path is up to
us. We might as well feel the best that we can and live with quality in times of adversity.

This book is not about unhappiness, but I want to deal with
the tough stuff up front. We all know life has pain and disappointment as well as pleasure. Bad things happen, really bad
things, and it is absurd to say that we can be happy about them.
But there are ways of dealing well with these things that will

increase the chances of deeper happiness in the future instead of adding to the suffering of an already painful situation. I believe that we can hold on to our happiness even during the rough patches.

When we're called to face an awful situa-tion, we need to tap our inner resources, already in place, ready to be put to use. We need to keep nourishing and replenishing ourselves in tough times. Painful times in our lives are, in effect, emotional marathons, and we know marathon runners don't run on empty. We need to be in training in order to be at our strongest, most courageous best. When we exhibit grace under fire, we will experience and face up to pain, but we will get through whatever is required of us. No matter how painful the situation, we're never disconnected from the source of our strength; we're always lifted up by love.

> *Why cling to the pain and the wrongs of yesterday? Why hold on to the very things that keep you from hope and love?*
>
> BUDDHA

We can't always be happy about what happens, but we can be pleased with the way we handle ourselves and cope. We should focus our energy on how we react to circum-stances beyond our control, not on why something painful has happened. Accept the truth. Whatever can't be changed has to be accepted, just as it is. When we bravely face truth, we use our energies to do whatever good we can. We listen and hear, we look and see the many constructive ways we can be useful.

> *I never fight . . . except against difficulties.*
>
> HELEN KELLER

you'll never walk alone

We must face many of our difficulties in our own ways, on our own terms. Everyone has a different style of coping with the tough stuff. As for me, I've always found that I heal most quickly when I reach out to others in loving ways. We are together, not alone. I can lend a hand, a kiss, write a note, listen, be present, smile. At Mayor John V. Lindsay's triumphal memorial service, the expressive singer Patti LuPone sang a musical tribute, *You'll Never Walk Alone.* Peter and I had some friends over to our home afterward, and we talked about our friend John, remembering happy times shared. We needed to be together, not alone. We needed to feel the connections of one human life linked to so many others. In sad times, our hearts expand when we're consciously present to our connectedness, one person to another.

> *Healing begins with caring.*
>
> BILL MOYERS

happy-sad

All of us go through hard times; no one is exempt. Together we can maintain some level of happiness as best we can, elevating each other, being gentle, reaching out in loving ways, bringing hope and comfort. We can develop a happiness formula for ourselves that works in the good times and that helps guide and encourage us in the sad, low times. Our practice of happiness redirects our energy,

> *Happiness can only be felt if you don't set any conditions.*
>
> ARTHUR RUBINSTEIN

bringing light and sunshine bursting through the dark clouds. The happiness is there, just as the sun is, but it is temporarily clouded over.

The inevitable tough times are equivalent to driving through a dark, slippery tunnel in a bad storm. Rationally, you know that there is light at the end. You're prepared for the dark. You turn on your bright lights, you make sure your seatbelt is fastened, and you drive slowly and steadily. You concentrate. You have to be particularly cautious, because you can't move to the left or the right or backward. You must keep to the line and gradually move forward, carefully and methodically. How long will it take to get through this dark place and space? As long as it takes to safely move ahead in the right direction, doing the best you can under less than desirable circumstances.

When you are going through a difficult time, do the things you know work to lift your spirits and sustain you. Challenging times require more positive energy, more affirmations, tenderness, and attention. During these hard times, we must take time to listen to our bodies. When we have all the ingredients for living well in place, we go through the hoops a lot better prepared. We intuitively look for any signs of light that will illuminate our path.

We will, from time to time, be happy-sad. There are whole areas in our life that are uplifting and nourish us while we are facing a tough situation. We have a wealth of positive resources that come to our aid. In times of crisis, we need to teach ourselves continuously to strengthen our inner world. Through regular rituals,

The word "happiness" would lose its meaning if it were not balanced by sadness.

CARL JUNG

The butterfly counts not months but moments and has time enough.

RABINDRANATH

TAGORE

disciplines, and private ceremonies, we become more centered and therefore more courageous. We feel our inner strength coming to our aid. The more deeply conscious we are of the present moment, the clearer our vision of inner transformation.

be prepared

The formulas and strategies we apply when everyone is fine and everything is running smoothly are more necessary than ever when painful or challenging situations arise or we are going through a low period. We need a clear-cut plan of action that keeps us focused on our intentions. What do you do under normal conditions to boost your mood? We have to intentionally remind ourselves of what increases our good energy, what steps we can take to get through specific situations with as much intelligence and order as possible.

Lock your house, go across the railroad tracks and find someone in need and do something for him.

KARL MENNINGER'S ADVICE TO A MAN WHO SAID HE WAS GOING TO HAVE A NERVOUS BREAKDOWN

In troubled times, our mind tends either to relive the trauma and dwell on tragic details, or to race ahead, skipping over it. Stay aware in the present. Rather than spacing out or avoiding reality, we can muster enormous courage by being in tune with what is actually happening now. Observe your thoughts. Listen to what is going on.

Whether you are ill or someone you love is going through a tough time, take one step at a time. Take one deep breath at a time. Slow down your pace. Watch your thoughts and emotions carefully. Slowly, determine what is the best way to take care of what needs to be done. Write a list, be as specific as possible. Be determined to act as an instrument of your own healing.

Whether you're involved in a lawsuit, have been in an automobile accident, have a sick child or a spouse who has been diagnosed with an illness, your goal is to do your best and do whatever is required of you right now. When we care enough to do our best moment to moment, we're healing our own pain. Take care of now, this very moment. Continue to do this, one hour at a time, one day at a time. You will move through your situation as well as humanly possible when you focus on each minute, and view it as a fresh opportunity to point to your own light. By facing the tough stuff well, remaining positive, thinking of all your blessings and focusing on the smaller areas of your life you have some control over, you begin to transcend your pain.

Happiness is really caring and being able to do something about the caring.

BRIAN O'CONNELL

transcending pain

Our painful experiences strengthen us in becoming more empathetic, more caring, and deeper human beings. We grow in depth of understanding, with greater appreciation for the miracle of life. We all have our struggles. None of us is spared. Pain is inevitable. We try to learn from our experiences how to move our energy into more pure, positive directions. We must remain focused on our goals so that our light shines as brightly as

One kind word can warm three winter months.

JAPANESE SAYING

Man is now only more active—not more happy —not more wise, than he was six thousand years ago.

EDGAR ALLEN POE

possible in situations that require our inner strength.

How many times have you been able to transform pain by intensely paying attention to your inner world? When we are fully conscious, accepting what we cannot change, taking responsibility for what we can, windows of opportunity open up.

crying

Often, when I cry, a transformation of spirit takes place and I'm able to let go of the pain. A few hours after Powell died, I called my spiritual mentor, John Coburn. Just hearing his soft-spoken "hello" made me burst into tears. He couldn't even tell who was on the other end of the line. "Who is this?" he inquired, probably inclined to think someone had dialed the wrong number. I gulped, took a deep breath, and said, "John, it's Alexandra. Do you have a minute to talk?" He obviously felt my distress and said yes. I told him that Powell had never recovered from open-heart surgery. Because John knew my family well, it was a comfort to me to speak with him. The reality was so alive, death is so final. Today, Powell wasn't dying, he was dead. As helpful as the doctors and nurses were, Powell was a case, a patient, a stranger, someone whose heart needed repairing and it hadn't quite worked out.

The secret of contentment is knowing how to enjoy what you have, and to be able to lose all desire for things beyond your reach.

LIN YUTANG

Having someone to talk to, a person you

greatly respect, someone you love, who loves you, can be a real comfort in times of great need. Recognize the healing power of the presence and understanding of a caring friend and teacher. Months later, John teased me, "Alexandra, I've reread several of your books and I don't see that you've written anything about crying."

Having a good cry can help us to heal. We can feel sad about what is happening or has happened and then move back into the present moment. Breaking down in tears over a seriously painful event is perfectly natural and healthy. Think of your tears as a sign of your compassion and love. Allow yourself to be fully present to the pain. Feel your emotions. Observe your thoughts. Your tears will help to heal your broken heart. Let your vulnerability be your strength. Tears of sorrow cleanse your soul. Crying is a sign of acceptance. You face the pain, you feel it in your body, you observe it in your mind and emotions. Crying doesn't last long. You catch yourself, realizing it is now time to let go and move on.

So to yield to life is to solve the unsolvable.

LAO TSU

the breath of life

Throughout my adult life, I have tried to pay attention to my breathing. There are moments when breathing consciously is all we can do for ourselves. Our breathing is the best way to be in close touch with our bodies, because this is our immediate way to know how we are managing our inner space. When

Cannot we let people be themselves, and enjoy life in their own way?

EMERSON

The highest service we can perform for others is to help them help themselves.

HORACE MANN

we are conscious of our breathing, we feel more alive, more vibrant. I was an eager athlete growing up, and tennis was my favorite sport. I learned to inhale deeply as the ball came to me and deeply exhale as I hit the ball. When we are aware of our breathing, we are conscious of not taking our life force for granted. When I fill my lungs with fresh air, inhaling deeply and exhaling fully my consciousness expands. The present becomes more spacious, timeless, complete. There are many good books on breathing techniques that may help to reduce stress caused by a past- or future-focused mind. If you have never paid serious attention to breathing, I recommend that you buy one or two of these books and practice some of the useful techniques that help us to stay centered in the moment.

Throughout the day, I perform hundreds of mini breathing rituals that gradually put me in closer touch with my whole body. When I pass a table with a bouquet of fresh flowers, I put my nose right up to them and inhale their fragrance. Conscious breathing allows us to soak it all in, taking time to smell the roses. I inhale deeply when I open the back door of the cottage to a sunny day and breathe in the fresh air and light. Our lungs are happy, our heart is delighted, and we feel opened up to absorb more life force flowing through our bodies. Each moment gives us a fresh breath of air, an opportunity to take heart, to face reality, and bravely move on.

Weeping may endure for a night, but joy cometh in the morning.

PSALM 30

not telling everyone about our pain

When I am moving through a difficult situation, I find I am better off if I am private about it, not sharing it with others. Some painful situations are private. Often, confiding in one or two intimates is all you really need to do.

Telling others about our pain puts too much energy out there that is negative and not constructive. Friends and family, no matter how well meaning, often can't keep a secret. They tell their friends and so add to the burden. We can't go into every detail, because it drags our energy down. When we're faced with a challenge, our energy should be spent getting through it as well as possible. Doing so requires acceptance and moving forward. Rather than externalizing a situation by talking about it, it is more powerful and healing to go inward to your radiant consciousness and do your inner work. If you choose to tell someone besides a spouse, a child, or a significant other, choose carefully. You may decide you need counseling. Think through your needs, what is best for you, who can be most helpful.

Our culture resonates in tense times to individual acts of grace.

JENNIFER JAMES

Because pain is a normal, natural part of human life, when we're willing to accept it and try to move through it, we'll want to live as normal a life as we can, carrying on our responsibilities as well as possible. Feeling the genuine love of friends when I'm facing a painful period is sustaining. I can laugh and have fun because the energy is positive. This alone is healing. Learning about their lives, their work, and their families transports me out of my unpleasant situation, giving me a refreshing taste of normal life.

Assume that everyone you know, as well as strangers, is going through a hard time. The odds will be with you. Realization of others' suffering cultivates your compassion. Your smile, your gentleness, your caring about others' dignity and well-being will help strengthen them in their self-healing process, just as the same empathy from others helps you to be brave.

Love—the more you share with others, the more you have.

MOTHER TERESA

The worst mistake anyone can make is to feel self-pity. It causes a spiral of negative energy that tears down rather than builds up. We all know how damaging self-pity is.

two salads

Leaving the Chicago hospital after Powell died, Peter and I stepped outside onto a new blanket of snow. The sparkling snowflakes dancing in the quiet air refreshed me. We walked arm in arm in silence to a restaurant two blocks away, where we'd been with Powell many times. We sat at a small table by the window so we could look out at the snow. When the waiter asked me what I wanted for lunch, I ordered a field greens salad and a Cobb salad. He told me I was ordering two salads. "Don't you want to try the fish of the day or the roasted chicken?" "No, thank you. My brother just died and I want to have two salads. Thank you." We are sometimes intimidated by waiters, but I knew what I wanted and he served me two salads. A few tears fell as I envisioned Powell sitting at a nearby table, feeling his presence,

We could never learn to be brave and patient if there were only joy in the world.

HELEN KELLER

his laughter, his warm conversation, but Peter and I had a tender lunch together after a difficult, painful week. Being out with people who are having a good time helps us to keep the pain in its place and not fuel it. At that moment, I was sad-happy. Glad I loved my brother, grateful I'd been there for his operation, glad he would not have to suffer more pain.

Kind words produce their own image in men's souls; and a beautiful image it is.

BLAISE PASCAL

Peter and I felt blessed to have our health and each other. We talked about what needed to be done to help with a memorial service. We both decided we were emotionally wiped out and needed to go back to the hotel and have a nap. I picked up several bunches of tulips to make the hotel room more cheerful. We asked the hotel to save our phone messages for us and wake us up at four o'clock. In times of deep pain and shock, we can do simple things for ourselves that will help us to heal. The cozy white terrycloth robe felt comforting, the cool crisp white sheets were inviting. I went to sleep within seconds.

looking our best

We shouldn't let ourselves down when we're facing troubles. When we look our best we feel better. The outer informs the inner, because they are not separate, but one. The way we take care of our appearances can have a profound influence on our feelings.

Believe that you may understand.

SAINT AUGUSTINE

Some hospitals offer classes in "Look Pretty, Feel Well," where motivational speakers encourage the patients to wear makeup and use lotions, creams, and cologne. At the end of these talks, each patient is given a bag of free samples, donated by cosmetic companies.

Shallow men believe in luck or in circumstance. Strong men believe in cause and effect.

EMERSON

Both men and women can use a body moisturizer, some hand cream, a fragrant soap, and the men some fresh-smelling aftershave. The patients seem to respond positively to these classes and say that they feel better and that others notice their recovering spirit.

When you pay attention to your personal grooming, wearing clean, attractive bathrobes, slippers that fit well, and fresh pajamas or nightgowns, you feel life is good, because your energy is increased. Many people try to look good when they are going to be seen by others. I believe we should have a certain standard all the time, because how we dress affects how we ourselves look and feel and proves to be good for our health and self-healing.

Wear a freshly starched shirt even if you are not going to leave home. Wear polished shoes. Be mindful of your posture. The slightest positive thing you may do for yourself will increase your positive energy. Dress for happiness in trying times and see for yourself how greatly you're able to lift your spirits. Wear your favorite colors and watch how the beams of sunshine break through.

what comforts you?

After a friend was in an accident—a taxi she was riding in smashed into a car—her face was black and blue. She had scratches and some stitches on her nose. Her children, her three-month-old grandson, and her cocker spaniel comforted Jane as her bruises healed. She found pleasure in playing the piano and singing, and was grateful she survived the ordeal.

From the highest to the humblest tasks, all are of equal honor; all have their part to play.

WINSTON CHURCHILL

I have a friend who has learned that her father has been diagnosed with incurable cancer. After they had spent a tearful weekend together, talking about how much they love each other, what comforted her in the weeks and months that followed was to begin each new day writing a love poem to her dad. Her father told his daughter that he didn't want to talk about his illness; instead, he wanted to focus completely on living each moment to the hilt. He is thriving. Many studies confirm that love and caring cannot always cure, but they have the power to heal.

children

I enjoy being with my children even when I am in pain. We tell stories, bringing back good memories. They know better than anyone how to make me laugh at myself, lighten up, enjoy the fun of life. We may go to the movies, or go grooving together, or perhaps we'll shop for some needed boots or a pair of slacks, or they'll encourage me to buy a soft, sensuous, brightly colored bathrobe in a floral pattern to cheer me. We hold hands, we hug, and we have a good time focusing on each other. We get all dressed up for a dinner celebration at

Happiness depends more on the inward disposition of mind than on the outward circumstances.

BENJAMIN FRANKLIN

home in a good frame of mind. I can train myself to be in a present moment, in a happy state of awareness when I accept pain bravely. Children magically help us heal. They never fail to bring strength and joy.

staying connected to our true nature

In the crisis times of my life, I love being with my family and friends. I want to listen to beautiful music and have pretty flowers around me to provide a cheerful atmosphere. When going through a rough patch, it's important to be intensely aware of your own needs and the various ways you can heal yourself.

Character is the basis of happiness and happiness the sanction of character.

GEORGE SANTAYANA

What you most enjoy when you're feeling wonderful are the experiences that will lift your spirits when you're faced with temporary pain. The beach always has a great healing power. Swimming in the ocean, smelling the flowers, or walking in a garden keeps us grounded, reminding us of life's preciousness, nature's cycles, and love's eternal grace.

What I do to comfort myself when I'm in pain are things I love to do normally, when I'm thriving. Stay connected to your happier self, because it is right here with you wherever you are, whatever you are going through. Pay attention now. Review your ten words and be true to them.

the really bad stuff

There is always something constructive we can do to improve a situation, to find a way through the darkest times. We always have a choice about how we respond to the energy of a painful event. Everything continuously changes. We can be proactive and figure out ways of improving a situation, regardless how sad or tough. If you have a child in the hospital, no matter how devoted you are as a parent, the doctors may only let you see your child at certain prescribed times. When you know that you won't be able to see your son or daughter until parents are allowed back to visit, you have some choices to make. If there is a museum near the hospital, you could go there and wander around the exhibits. You may want to go to a coffee shop near the hospital or sit in a nearby park in the sun and write in your journal, peacefully read poetry, or write a note to a close friend.

It is one of the most beautiful compensations of this life that no man can sincerely try to help another without helping himself.

EMERSON

Getting away from the often depressing atmosphere of the hospital for an hour or several hours is healthy and gives you a fresh perspective, as well as fresh air and some natural light. You return more capable of providing positive inspiration and cheer.

There are times when nothing is gained by hanging around the waiting room. When my mother was dying in a hospital in Connecticut, my lifeline was the loving support of two dear friends. Tink and Pat took turns meeting me at the train station, taking me to their homes, giving me a soothing cup of tea, letting me admire their houses or allowing me quiet time in their gardens. They'd then drop me off at the hospital. I'd feel refreshed and ready to do whatever I could for my mother.

Even when we go through these difficult times, there is no need to be dreary. My mother looked forward to my positive energy, my good news about the family, and tales of her grandchildren. I brought flowers and photographs of the girls. I asked her questions about her childhood and her passions. I always tried to look my best by wearing bright, cheerful colors. My walking into her room was the big event of her day. Her eyes lit up when I greeted her and she always smiled. My presence alone seemed to lift her spirits. I wanted her to live with the best quality of life even though she was confined to bed. Flowers were sacred to my mother as they are to me, and I knew how to please her. I saw to it that the sterile hospital room where she spent the better part of the final year of her life was a garden in full bloom. By my creating a garden in her room, visitors were cheered up as well, and there was a noticeable effect on the staff. They seemed to like to see and experience the cheerful garden.

> *Every human being has a great . . . gift to care, to be compassionate, to be present to the other, to listen, to hear, and to receive.*
>
> HENRI J. NOUWEN

being with deeply unhappy people

Love and the golden rule guide us in our dealings with unhappy people. Sometimes we have to be with people we don't choose to be with. No matter how much we relish life or how positive our energy, there will be unpleasant entangle-ments. We all have them. How we handle our emotions when we're in these situations is what matters.

In about the same degree as you are helpful you will be happy.

THEODORE REIK

It is natural to choose to be around happy people who energize us, are fun to be with, who inspire us to be our best. From experi-ence, however, we know that not every relationship will be mutually beneficial or productive. When we encounter a situa-tion that is potentially debilitating, we can accomplish our goal to cause no harm to others or ourselves by keeping our integrity and maintaining our code of behavior. We have to continu-ously be aware that we are responsible for keeping our thoughts pure and our actions wholesome and constructive. What we don't admire in another's conduct, we must be sure not to be guilty of ourselves.

Despondent, complaining people can drain us of our vital-ity, test our code of happiness, and wear down our soul. The Pulitzer Prize–winning author Toni Morri-son no longer rushes to everyone's aid. "I have to care for the juices, the generosity, the emo-tional energy that I have," she writes. The philosopher and author Tom Morris goes so far as to say that you should "associate as much as you can with the people of admirable char-acter because we become like the people we're around."

It had done me good to be somewhat parched by the heat and drenched by the rain of life.

HENRY WADSWORTH

LONGFELLOW

The Dalai Lama tries to be kind and compassionate to every person he meets. We can also try to do this. All that is ever expected of us is to do our best under all circumstances, not just in the easy situations. The challenge is to face the truth, to get through difficulties, to remain tender and loving to each other.

"i smile"

A salesperson at Nordstrom's in Philadelphia told me recently that the only people who get her down are the ones who are negative. "They make me unhappy. I can deal with the sick, the lost, the misled, those who have difficult problems, but miserable people cause most of the problems." When I asked her how she manages to be around these negative people, she said, "I smile. I keep smiling. It always softens someone. They become less negative." A pleasant smile helps in every situation. A smile connects one spirit to another.

To glorify the past and paint the future is easy, to survey the present and emerge with some light and understanding is difficult.

LIN YUTANG

The opposite of a frown is a warm smile. This simple gesture can help bring someone else's energy up while not taking ours away. The modern-day saint Mother Teresa advised us, "Let us always meet each other with a smile, for the smile is the beginning of love." A smile, like love, is always appropriate, helpful, and caring. A gentle opposing energy can bring balance, just as love counters hate. Remain sensitive to others' emotional pain as you try to cheer them up, telling some upbeat stories or news. If you have a good sense of humor, tell a light joke or two to try to make them laugh.

Try to look sincerely for the best in every person. Good is

there; it is up to us to find it. We can extend goodness even when people are irrational. "Avoid a negative argument," Norman Vincent Peale advised, "but whenever a negative attitude is expressed, counter with a positive and optimistic opinion."

Use the law of opposites thought by thought. When there is confusion, show understanding; when there is discouragement, show encouragement; when a person shows disdain, be sympathetic.

In times of need, one should rise to the occasion and fight bravely for what is right.

DALAI LAMA

limits

Try to set up a visit with a difficult person on your own terms. Whenever possible, choose to be in a cheerful, familiar, colorful atmosphere where you feel good energy. Choose to keep the visits to a limited time. Your goal is to do the right thing, but there is no benefit to overdoing. Remind yourself that no one can ever substantially change another person. We are ultimately responsible for our own thoughts, actions, and choices. Don't force an emotional relationship with people you choose not to become close to. Let them be. They have their own lives to lead, their own inner work to do. The people you're obliged to be with from time to time should not become a source of guilt. We can't be someone else's savior.

The burden is sometimes lightened by sharing it. If your spouse has a difficult father, your presence during the visit may be helpful.

Those who bring sunshine to the lives of others cannot keep it from themselves.

JAMES MATTHEW

BARRIE

We all want to be happy, and we're all going to die . . .
the only two unchangeable true facts that apply to every human being on this planet.

WILLIAM BOYD

You will be demonstrating your love for your husband, whose father will benefit from experiencing your connectedness and your caring energy. Whenever you join with someone you have a healthy relationship with, your positive energy is always stronger than the negative energy of the person you're visiting. Keep focused on the reason you are having this encounter. If it is to be supportive to someone you love, you'll be better able to maintain your positive energy.

polish your mirror

I try to keep the words of the thirteenth-century Persian poet Rumi in mind when someone finds fault with and is disparaging toward me: "Your criticism polishes my mirror." Be silent. Listen. Watch your thoughts. Be alert to exactly what you are thinking. When there are negative patterns, you don't need to get hooked into negative responses. Wait to reply. Be still. Concentrate on your breathing. Accept what may be truthful in what's been said without losing your dignity or composure.

a professional's advice

I had a rewarding talk with Martha H. Bush, a psychotherapist and clinical social worker, about the best ways to prepare one-

self for being with difficult people. We discussed how to practice self-preservation without hurting the other person.
When we are in a troublesome situation, she advises us to try
to be our own best self. If you are provoked,
don't allow the attack to hurt you. If you
believe in angels, envision your guardian
angel protecting you. When there is a difficult interaction, be on your best behavior, be
honest without being hurtful. Don't allow
yourself to be pulled down by someone. Bol-
ster yourself by remembering that you want
to do the right thing, to be kind. Keep clearly
in your mind that you can't control another's
behavior; you can only control your response.

No matter what you are doing, keep the undercurrent of happiness. Learn to be secretly happy within your heart in spite of all circumstances.

PARAMAHANSA

YOGANANDA

Martha Bush suggests that we find the
middle ground so we are neither a victim nor an aggressor. If
someone is nasty, angry, and loses control, attacking us, we can
tell them that we feel that they are angry. Or, "It sounds like
you are angry about losing your job," or, "It sounds like you're
angry about the divorce." These words tend to diffuse their
anger and cause them to focus on what is actually making them
unhappy.

live each day

We can feel the power of our own light even in the dark
times. The time to be aware of our life force is always now.
We can live each day as though it were our first and our last.

You cannot make yourself feel something you do not feel, but you can make yourself do right in spite of your feelings.

PEARL S. BUCK

We greet each morning with the freshness of a child; we feel the awesome beauty in the gift of being able to experience this present moment fully. If we live each day as though it were our last, what would we choose to do to bring more meaning and purpose to our lives here on earth? What would we think, feel, and do to make ourselves smile, to feel happy, to experience joy? I have faith that there will never be anything we will have to face that will overwhelm us.

PART II

happiness day by day

CHAPTER 5

paradise on earth

Happiness comes from within, and rests most securely on simple goodness and clear conscience . . . to make another happy is to be happy oneself.

—WILLIAM OGDON

Appreciation is a wonderful thing, it makes what is excellent in others belong to us as well.

—VOLTAIRE

my big discovery

The secret of happiness is that it is always a choice. I was fortu-nate to learn this early on. I was never one to play with dolls or to play house. The real world was far more exciting to me. When I was five years old, my parents moved from Weston, Massachusetts, to Westport, Connecticut, my father having accepted a job offer in New York City. My mother immediately joined a local garden club; it was an opportunity for her to meet new friends and share a passion for the garden. I was excited about the idea of starting my own garden club once I learned there weren't any garden clubs for children. My mother responded receptively because she thought starting a club would be a good opportunity for me to meet new friends. I learned that you have to decide what you're enthusiastic about, what you prefer to do, in order to have it manifest in your life.

When we are young, we have to ask an adult's permission in order to obtain our heart's desire. If I hadn't been bursting with excitement and anticipation, literally jumping for joy, I never would have been taken seriously. My happiness and enthusiasm were contagious. My mother was really quite delighted, even though she often had to carpool the girls as well as let her flowerbeds become a cutting garden for the bouquets we created. We'd tie the cut flowers with her ribbons and sell them door-to-door at inflated prices.

Two years later, my parents leased a small farmhouse in a rural part of upstate New York, where we went in the summer months. Surrounded by fields, I was inspired to have my own garden, where I intended to grow flowers, fruits, and vegetables. When

> *Our own interests are still an exquisite means for dazzling our eyes agreeably.*
>
> BLAISE PASCAL

> *Give me books, fruit, French wine and fine weather and a little music out of doors, played by someone I do not know.*
>
> JOHN KEATS

I asked my parents if I could have a garden of my own, they agreed as long as I would be personally responsible for cultivating and maintaining it. These experiences as a young child made me aware that happiness doesn't just come upon us automatically; we have to choose it and reach out and grasp it.

The discovery of a new dish does more for human happiness than the discovery of a new star.

ANTHELME BRILLAT-SAVARIN

I'm sure some of my passion for the garden was nurtured by my mother and her best friend, my godmother, Mitzi. When we are young we want to emulate grownups we love and admire. However, what might begin innocently as a way to enjoy intimacy and connection with loved ones may grow into our own meaningful experiences. No one literally planted the seeds of my own garden, but my elders' example and encouragement were inspiring. Certainly their own pretty gardens and their love of flowers and flower arranging inspired me, but there was definitely an inner spark, something internal that led to my own choices on my own, I chose to become a gardener, although I was grateful for the rich exposure to others' gardens.

These early experiences of certain strong urges, and encouragement in carrying out my desires, have led me on my path of focusing on what makes me happy, what increases my love of life. I was blessed in having my mother and Mitzi listen to my desires, because I now see clearly how one thing led to another: One choice opened the door to the next choice.

The environment is not a world—it is an individual thing.

SRI AUROBINDO

There is no doubt that the garden itself was also my teacher. I was in awe of the beauty of nature, the miracle of creation, the wonder of seeds being planted in the ground and producing colorful, fragrant flowers, fruits, and vegetables. I learned that when I tilled the soil, fertilized, watered, weeded, and pruned, growth unfolded and things ripened, sprouted, and blossomed.

Go into the sunshine and be happy with what you see.

WINSTON CHURCHILL

I learned about nature's rhythms, about patience and timing. I became attached to being in the fresh air, in the light, surrounded by living things I helped cultivate. There was so much to do, so much excitement. I seemed to have worked with an effortless ease, my happiness carrying me along as I filled the wheelbarrow with the fruits of my labor.

In the garden I learned to be mindful. I observed the patterns of the light, paid attention to what needed more of my care, as well as to what was thriving on benign neglect. I spent hours in quiet contemplation, envisioning the pretty colors appearing as vividly as on the seed packages I had stapled to posts to remind me what I'd planted and where. My first garden led me to jot down ideas in a spiral notebook, a habit that has lasted since then.

the importance of nourishing our physical world

The garden was my first teacher of the great significance of the effect of beauty in our lives. We must cultivate happiness in our external world. Our immediate environment is one large part of our lives we can control. How we nurture our lives through the choices we make about where we live, the mood, spirit, and energy of our house, the rooms we decorate and occupy, the food we eat, the rituals we perform, the clothes we wear, and the colors we select to uplift us, make up approximately half of our happiness. If we can improve our well-being by 50 percent, we should concentrate at least that much of our efforts on our external world, the one world we occupy by ourselves, the place where we live.

The good things of life are not to be had singly, but come to us with a mixture.

CHARLES LAMB

becoming fully present

We should always follow our hearts. When we're mindful of what we love, where we most love to be, who we love to be with, how we enjoy spending our time, we have the key to living wisely. Often, after I've listened to music for a while, I enjoy the silence. I sit still in a chair, shut my eyes, and breathe deeply. There is a sweetness in the atmosphere. I hear the gentle tick of the grandfather clock, the squeak and hiss of the crackling fire, the laughter of the girls upstairs. I inhale the spicy smell of curry sauce simmering in the kitchen. I smile as the scent of baking chocolate chip cookies mingles with the spices, the curry and ginger.

where art is living

I open my eyes and see all the pretty colors around me, colors I've intentionally chosen to make me happy. I look around at our cheerful paintings. Each one brings me to a refreshing scene of sky, water, and cottages, as well as tables with flowers and food.

A happy childhood is one of the best gifts that parents have in their power to bestow.

MARY CHOLMONDELEY

These pictures are windows thrown wide open to sunny places in Provence that overlook the Mediterranean. I'm invigorated by the clarity of the pure colors and the simple beauty of the physical environment. While I don't live in the South of France, the energy and spirit of our paintings enhance our lives day to day.

These simple paintings remind me to reach out for all the natural beauty possible. The paintings of interiors, for example, are exuberant with flowers on tablecloths, with fruit in a bowl, a bottle of port wine, an open window sweeping a yellow tablecloth into the air, the light of out of doors. They remind me that our rooms can inspire us, uplift us, encourage our enthusiasms, and feed our passions. The rooms in our homes can be lovely expressions of our love of life.

Whether a painting is of the outside, where we're looking at a simple cottage, or inside, feeling we're seated on a chair "at table," there is an exuberance of spirit, a celebration of the beauty of day-to-day life. Our awareness of all the happiness in the laughter of intimate conversation, the pleasure of sharing a delicious meal, the enjoyment of our domestic lives raises living to an art.

home as garden

Is there anything as sensuous or as beautiful as being outside in a garden in full bloom? We can think of our home as a lovely garden that we enjoy cultivating. Houses, like gardens, need our watchful eye, sunshine and nurturing. The houses where we live

don't thrive on benign neglect. Living abun-
dantly requires lots of loving energy.

Nothing here below is profane for those who know how to see.

Stay alert to what is giving you the greatest
pleasure now in your home. What do you want
to uproot and cart away because you no longer
appreciate it? What do you choose to add?

PIERRE TEILHARD

DE CHARDIN

Are there certain pieces of furniture that are too large in scale,
choking the space, detracting from the light, airy feeling of the
room? Now is the only time to see with fresh eyes. Our home,
just like our garden, evolves. We experiment, try out different
things and new colors until we feel content. Try to keep the
metaphor of home as garden in your consciousness. Feel everything around you as alive and vibrant. As we move along our
paths, we clearly see all the ways we can increase our happiness
day by day by having our homes become gardens in full bloom.

When we nourish our home with sunny, happy, garden-
fresh colors, sweet sounds, living plants, trees, and flowers;
when the energy is positive, when every wall,

Beauty is a gift.

every corner exudes light and charm, there is

ARISTOTLE

no need to have anything that is not meaning-
ful, useful, or beautiful. Our lives will speak for us. Let our
objects tell a happy story. Let the things we love point to our
reverence for beauty.

a gardener of life

Your home as a garden is a private refuge. This is the tiny space
you occupy and maintain on earth, your soil to cultivate. It is
sacred. Make your home a garden so breathtakingly beautiful

Taking the first footstep with a good thought, the second with a good word, and the third with a good deed, I entered Paradise.

ZOROASTER

that you inspire happiness in everyone you welcome in. When you plan and plant a garden, you become co-creator. You can have an indoor window box or a ledge where you garden in pots. Each one of us needs to be a gardener of life, because it is in nature that we live in constant wonder, in awe of the miracle of life.

When you need inspiration, pick up a picture book of Claude Monet's beloved home and garden at Giverny. Monet inspires because of his love of nature, his opening our eyes to the miraculous beauty around us, his love of delicious food, great conversation, and hard work in pursuit of his passion. We might not have Monet's talent for painting masterpieces, but we can transform our personal environment into a sensuous, happy, colorful retreat, a place that is so pretty, so cheerful and pleasing, that our personal environment becomes our sanctuary.

tending your own garden

The life given us by nature is short, but the memory of a well-spent life is eternal.

CICERO

Plant your seeds and cultivate your own garden. Everyone who does so is wise, because happiness is centered here. Our house becomes a home when we love it. Our home can always be in bloom, full of springtime, fresh beginnings, plants growing, and happiness flowering.

Paradise is right here, right now, day by day. The Chinese believe that what is below is equal in value to what is above. Our homes are our ideal earthly paradise. Give your home your all, feed it with beauty, color, and light; treat all your objects with respect and dignity, knowing you are only a tempo- rary caregiver.

Love . . . delights in what it looks at; and at its purest, it recognizes no higher purpose than delight.

DEEPAK CHOPRA

Every day we can live ideally. Wherever we are, wherever we go, we are grounded in the moment. It is here that we create paradise; it is here that we are nourished by our sacred refuge, our physical environment we love that loves us back. I think we often leave home just to have the thrill of returning to paradise on earth, our garden homes. Our homes can be so enriching that we choose not to leave at all and to take our vacations there.

flower budget

Because of my lifelong passion for the garden, I've made a commitment to myself to always have flowers around because of their powerful hold over me. I've managed my flower budget by having a flower fund, money I set aside each week for flowers. Sometimes I go over the budget; sometimes I don't use it all up, but there is money for flowers just as there is for food. I made the choice to be happier by living with colorful flowers in the rooms I occupy with family and friends. The pleasure of living with flowers, like most others, is shared.

Whether people are fully conscious of this or not, they actually derive countenance and sustenance from the "atmosphere" of the things they live in and with.

FRANK LLOYD WRIGHT

Dwell upon what is most lovable about a person who is most loving in your life today.

DEEPAK CHOPRA

My choice is not whether to have flowers, but rather what kind, depending on the season, cost, and availability. Our backyard at the cottage is so tiny that I usually grow roses in pots. I buy most of the cut flowers we have inside the house or apartment, although we have friends who are great gardeners and bring us roses, peonies, and dahlias in the summer months. I've had excellent luck at the A&P supermarket as well as at the fruit, flower, and vegetable markets in New York City. Going downtown to the flower market early in the morning is a treat I indulge in about once a month. In order not to end up in the poorhouse, I discipline myself not to go overboard when I'm there, because the temptation of a variety of fresh flowers from all over the world is extraordinary.

One flower, when we're really able to see its beauty, connects us to all of nature. Flowers are a metaphor, continuously reminding me who I am, what makes me comfortable, what increases my love of life, and what I value in the rooms where we live. Clearly, having a beautifully decorated home is not enough. The entire message is always about living. When we identify what increases our happiness, we will want to nurture and nourish the things that are so much a part of us.

Flowers are the sweetest things God ever made.

HENRY WARD

BEECHER

Making this commitment to my passion over all these years has helped me to stay in touch with my happier power. When we do things to remind ourselves of the natural beauty of this earth, we are more mindful of what matters most to us. By having flowers in a bud vase or in a large bouquet, I can visualize gardens—my own from my past as well as friends' gardens, gardens I see along country roads, and famous gardens open to the public on tours. If a garden is paradise on earth and a place of ideal beauty, why not choose to be co-creator and live in a garden every day?

go ahead and sneeze

Brooke surprised Peter and me by bringing a huge bouquet of tightly packed roses when she joined us for dinner at a French bistro near her apartment. "Happy early Valentine's Day," she said. The roses had been props on a television set for *House & Garden*, where she works, and they would have died if they had been left in the hot office building over the weekend. The floral artist had arranged a rainbow of colors from white to yellow to peach, orange, pinks of all shades, purples, and reds. The bouquet was "over the top," with dozens of beautiful, colorful roses. Everyone in the restaurant smiled. Some wanted to know what the occasion was. "Happy birthday?" "Happy anniversary?" "What is the cause for celebra-tion?" Waiters bent down to smell the roses. Everyone leaving the restaurant passed our table and bent down to touch, smell and admire them in such a happy mood. The roses stole the show. This bouquet was so joyful, there wasn't anyone who was blasé. One woman cupped her hands over the roses, shut her eyes, and smiled in silent reverie, absorbing their positive

Tenderness . . . the joy of being friendly, of being warm, of considering and respecting another person and of making this other person happy.

ERICH FROMM

energy. She is a healer. She mused, almost to herself, "If more people lived with fresh flowers every day when they felt well, I believe there would be less illness."

I've never met a man who didn't love flowers. Flowers, like love, don't belong only to one sex. If I were allergic to certain flowers, I'd go ahead and sneeze before I'd give up living with them. My experience in the restaurant that Friday evening illustrated to me the universal sense of happiness that nature's color and beauty brings to us. The special occasion is always today, always now. If you're allergic to certain flowers and you sneeze, worse things could happen. Taking time to smell the roses is the central message. Peter's mother always sneezed when she tasted chocolate, but that never kept her from having her favorite sweet every evening after dinner. If you occasionally sneeze because of a flower, this is a small price to pay for loving them, paying homage to what creates paradise on earth.

Who is the happiest of man? He who values the merits of others and in their pleasure takes joy.

GOETHE

light the lights

When we bought our old house in Connecticut, and I tried to grow a flower garden under the umbrella of a huge old maple tree, I had to re-learn a basic lesson: Flowers, to thrive, need more than good soil, fertilizer, water, and tender loving care; they need sunlight. This is so obvious, and something I knew well from early experience. There were no trees anywhere near my childhood garden because it was in the middle of a

What we love we shall grow to resemble.

SAINT BERNARD

wheat field. If the sun was shining, it shined on what I'd planted. In our tiny backyard in Connecticut, I wanted both the tree and the garden, but it didn't work. I had to choose one or the other. Human beings, like gardens, are also part of nature, and cannot thrive without sufficient sunlight. The sun sustains our life. We have to become more acutely aware of the crucial effect light has on our sense of happiness.

Life is a paradise for those who love many things with a passion.

LEO BUSCAGLIA

light is happiness

Be generous with your lighting. Light is happiness. When you are inside, you are deprived of 90 percent of the light you would experience if you were outside on a sunny July day under the shade of a tree or an umbrella. Because the sun moves, your windows are not constantly exposed to bright light even when it is sunny outside. Claude Monet's paintings teach us beautifully how fleeting natural light is. Have lots of backup lighting at home to boost your mood.

The fault-finder will find fault even in paradise.

HENRY DAVID

THOREAU

We are all light-deprived in one way or another. I tell my clients that if they don't have enough light in a room for plants to blossom, they are not getting enough light themselves. Think of yourself as a hothouse flower. We have to turn on our emotional growth lights. Well-lit rooms literally shed light on life. They invite, cheer, and welcome us, illuminating all the objects we love. When lights are on, we're more tempted to move around our house freely, doing different projects in different spaces.

Different places on the face of the earth have different vibrations . . . the spirit of place is a great reality.

D. H. LAWRENCE

To achieve high levels of happiness, reach for brightness in your daily life. Light and dark are integral to the natural cycle of life. We can accept darkness as we point toward the light. Become conscious of all your varied options for increasing the cheerfulness of your immediate surroundings. We know firsthand that the sun does not perpetually shine down on us. Not only do we face darkness every evening but there are also many overcast, dark, and stormy days. It is up to us to bring light into our lives. A sunny disposition is encouraged in a light, colorful, joyful atmosphere.

new lighting

At the hardware store, look into all the new lighting technology and equipment that use full spectrum lights. They simulate sunlight. Use under-cabinet lights in the kitchen to better illuminate the countertops. Put ceiling lights on a dimmer switch, so that you can dim them during candlelit dinners. Use floor cans with faceted bulbs like cut diamonds, and spread light upward to wash a wall with light. These cans are excellent for hiding behind a tree pot to light up the branches and cast shadows on the wall.

The foolish man seeks happiness in the distance; the wise grows it under his feet.

JAMES OPPENHEIM

Almost all art needs specific lighting. A picture light hung from the top of the frame is simple and does the job nicely. If you have a fine work of art, you can have a projector light recessed in the ceiling that illuminates the canvas precisely. There are many small recessed halogen spots you can have installed in the ceiling that rotate like a ball in a socket and can be aimed at a painting, a piece of sculpture, a bouquet of flowers, or a framed photograph of a loved one.

Beauty is the mystery which enchants us . . . beauty is dynamic.

ROLLO MAY

A single recessed halogen light fixture over the kitchen table, the sink, the dining room table, or a desk or an upholstered reading chair can make a huge difference by inviting us to use the spaces more frequently with more enjoyment. Decorative table lights add sweetness to a desk or an end table but often don't provide enough bright light. They restrict the wattage we can use; you don't want to singe the lampshade. Painted tin shades are safe but block a lot of light.

treasured objects

Objects we treasure bring us great happiness. I feel true reverence for beautiful man-made things. When we are charmed by an object, we form a strong connection with it that helps us achieve our own light. Treasured objects speak louder than words about who we are and what we value and hold dear.

Nature gives to every time and season some beauties of its own.

CHARLES DICKENS

We are never alone or lonely when we're surrounded by things we're emotionally attracted to, because they become close friends. We miss them when we go on a vacation or business trip. One of the joys of returning home is to be greeted by these faithful objects of our desire.

Our books, collections of inkwells, paperweights, and pens symbolically speak of a love of writing; our art speaks of our love of life. A collection of bells makes us mindful of the miracle of the moment when we ring them. A group of carriage clocks ticking and striking unites us with our heartbeat now. A collection of children's chairs makes us smile, as we always have a special place for children to sit. Quilts provide us with emotional comfort as well as aesthetic beauty.

The sunlight is one and the same wherever it falls, but only bright surfaces . . . can reflect it fully.

SRI RAMAKRISHNA

Move your treasured objects around. This way you will continuously see them with fresh, loving eyes. There is never only one place for an object. You can put a blue and white handblown glass rolling pin on a living room table if it looks pretty there. Let your spirit move you.

The objects we love will also be appreciated by family and friends. The treasuring of objects sublimely connects us to people and places from all over the world and are timeless remembrances of the power beauty has on our emotions.

nothing small goes unnoticed

Taking care of little things can make large improvements. If the latch on the front gate needs some 3-in-1 oil to make it easier to open and close, it is a grace note to take care of this small matter. If I open the cabinet under the sink and find a disaster area, sitting down on the kitchen floor and throwing away all the dried-up, no-longer-useful things and straightening up the space brings a sense of order, satisfaction, and pleasure.

Look around with fresh eyes. Tenderly smile at your new spaces, slowly moving around until you see something that needs to be loved up. If there is some chipped paint on your front door, touching it up will only take a few minutes. I suggest to clients that they always have at least a pint of paint for touchups for each room, clearly labeled "walls," "ceiling," "trim." If an old farm table has some white rings from wet glasses, a spot remover rubbed into the blemished wood really works to remove these unsightly marks.

Music produces a kind of pleasure which human nature cannot do without.

CONFUCIUS

Rather than glossing over little irritations, realize that they are areas in our lives we can do something about immediately. If the white embroidered curtains in your bathroom look dirty, throw them in the washing machine with some strong bleach, let them dry for a minute or two, and use some heavy spray starch when you iron them. When you hang them up again, you'll do double thumbs up to see how they illuminate the room. You'll realize how easy and fun it is to make a simple improvement.

In time, by fixing the small things around the house, we gain a sense of mastery. We realize that we can continuously make things better. Whether we sew on a loose button or use an old toothbrush to clean the grouting around the kitchen sink, taking care of these details brings us enormous satisfaction. The energy is always in the action. Look at something and say, yes, I can make it better. In a notebook, keep a list of improvements you want to make

Touch the earth, love the earth, honor the earth, her plains, her valleys, and her seas; rest your spirit in her solitary places.

HENRY BESTON

I am filled with a sense of sweetness and wonder that such little things can make a mortal so exceedingly rich.

THEODORE PARKER

in your house or apartment that you cannot make right now. Whether it is having the leak repaired in your bedroom or buying some blue paint for the bathroom ceiling, you will enjoy attending to what needs your help as soon as you have the time or money to do so.

It may be a chair seat that needs re-caning or a lamp that needs repairing or a chandelier that needs cleaning. Nothing is too little or too insignificant to deserve your attention. Treat the small things with great importance, because everything breathes the same air. We want the atmosphere in our home to be fresh and invigorating like a sunny spring day.

the joys of dining

Food is essential to our pleasure. Whenever we gather with family and friends, we serve or are offered food and drinks. When we desire paradise on earth, we can treat our daily meals as memorable banquets. We are now at the table, experiencing the feast. A favorite painting of mine shows a tablescape after an outdoor banquet. You're invited to sit "at table" and enjoy fruit, cheese, a sweet, and some wine. We love seeing this scene hanging in our study to whet our appetite for life as we sit at our desks and work.

Pleasure is the most real good in this life.

FREDERICK THE GREAT

In the intimacy of our home we can create the most attractive, sensuous meals when we dine by the glow of candlelight, arrange fresh flowers, and select pretty china, crystal, and

linens. Whenever I experience a beautifully served, sumptuous meal, I inhale life deeply in great appreciation, savoring every moment. I am mindful of my immediate happiness, my sense of completeness. We're given the amazing opportunity to regularly gather

Love many things.

VINCENT VAN GOGH

"at table" for the sacred ritual of coming together for meaning-ful conversation, toasts, laughter, and tears of joy. When the atmosphere is sweet, we feel more expansively open and loving. We feel the grace.

I'm grateful that food is a biological necessity, something we all need every day to produce our vital energy and maintain our life force. We are social animals. Breaking bread with people we love is one of the most enjoyable rituals human beings per-form.

The celebration, the ritual, and the ceremony surrounding food are just as important as the food itself. Subliminally we enjoy more than the flavors, smells, and textures. We are nour-ished by the beauty and intimacy and the love and joy of the tender moments shared. We are stimulated by the aesthetics of eating: the refinement of the silverware, the delicacy of

Beauty will save the world.

DOSTOYEVSKY

crystal wine glasses, the intricately hand-painted flowers on the dessert plates. Aesthetic qualities feed the human spirit and offer us color and variety as well as opportunities to feel grace notes of happiness.

food is a sensuous delight

On a scale of 1 to 10, how important is food to your sense of happiness? I like to joke that I've never missed a meal. (I recall having a fierce appetite for breakfast after the natural child-birth of both of my daughters.) I'm a great advocate of regarding food as pleasure as well as nourishment. When properly ritualized, eating is one of life's most enjoyable necessities.

Everyone chooses his love from the ranks of beauty according to his character.

PLATO

Studies confirm that we don't receive the same nutritional benefits from food eaten quickly as from food enjoyed as part of an aesthetic ritual. Aesthetics dignify our earthly journey.

Home is our emotional center, our sacred refuge, our private haven and our strength; but there are people to see, places to go, things to do away from home that we also love. If we're in a restaurant where the music is lively, where there are candles and flowers, where other people are celebrating, laughing, and having a great time together, it rubs off on us. We get in the swing of the moment, creating a memorably happy experience.

hunting and gathering

The joy of selecting the ingredients for our meals is not to be skipped over in the rush of life. Gathering things from different stores, selecting the cheeses, breads, fruits, and vegetables is a fun and integral part of the process of meal preparation. Whenever there is gathering, cooking, baking, and decorating, there is happiness.

When we set a pretty table with linens and our finest china, polished silver, and crystal stemmed glasses, dining by candlelight sets the stage for a most memorable, intimate dining occasion. I try never to do anything more attractively or elaborately for others because they are joining us "at table" than I would do for Peter and myself when we're home alone.

There is a blessing in the air.

WILLIAM
WORDSWORTH

the pleasure of cooking

Food is one of my ten defining words. On a scale from 1 to 10, how interested are you in food? Do you like to cook? I believe that creating a beautiful and delicious meal from start to finish for loved ones is one of the most satisfying uses of our time together. We use our hands and our hearts to whet our appetites for the feast to come.

I taught myself how to cook with the help of Julia Child, whose book *Mastering the Art of French Cooking* is a favorite. I've tried most recipes at least once. "If you can read," a friend told me when I was in my early twenties, "you can cook." Having learned the basics from my mother, who advised me to

Everything lives, everything is animated, everything seems to speak to me of my passion, everything invites me to cherish it.

ANNE DE LENCLOS

read *Joy of Cooking* from cover to cover, I went on to read other cookbooks. I've read so many recipes that I rarely measure ingredients anymore. I think I've absorbed the formulas.

dining alone

Life is too short to make an effort to dine beautifully only when we have extended family or friends present. Coming together to dine daily is essential to our happiness. We love going out to restaurants to enjoy the experience of eating with family and friends, but we also treasure having romantic dinners as a couple; this is what we do to keep romantic spirits uplifted.

The meaning of things lies not in the things themselves but in our attitude toward them.

ANTOINE DE
SAINT-EXUPÉRY

Those who live alone should remember to create an aesthetically pleasing experience that gives them pleasure. Each of us is worthy of a lovely, pleasant ritual at mealtime and teatime. I have friends who live alone and eat many meals in solitude. When we dine by ourselves, and we all do at times, we can be mindful of creating a table or tray that looks as pretty as it would if we had prepared it for loved ones. Play some favorite music, have flowers and candles, and sit peacefully in the beauty of your own home, absorbing all the good feelings. When we celebrate each meal as a vitally important ceremony, we will never feel alone. We'll all be, in effect, together, toasting each other "at table." Toast your friends, say a blessing, slowly enjoy a beautiful meal in the best of company.

Eating in solitude is a great opportunity to listen to our inner voice. If we eat a piece of bread slowly, we feel the sun and the rain that supported the wheat. Let your mindfulness open up your conscious awareness of how this food came to you. In joyful contemplation, see the big in the small, see and feel the connections.

diet and weight

If we ritualize each meal, never eating while standing, reading, or watching television or a video, not jumping up to answer the phone, or rushing, we can more easily maintain a stable weight over our lifetime. When we are in an attractive setting, eating small portions of a well-rounded meal, when we thoroughly chew our food before we swallow, we will feel satisfied after twenty minutes and seldom need more food. The beauty of our eating ritual calms us down as it lifts us up, and we are not inclined to overeat or overdrink. Happiness is derived from our mindful moderation.

Beauty is an ecstasy; it is as simple as hunger.

WILLIAM SOMERSET

MAUGHAM

easy ways to enhance your meals

Following is a list of things I've found useful to remember at mealtime:

❀ The flowers at the center of the table should be no higher than 12½ inches, the height of a cut daffodil, so that you

And those are the two things, tenderness and beauty.

D. H. LAWRENCE

don't create an emotional or visual barrier for the person across the table. The vase should be no higher than 6½ inches.

❀ When possible, have all the chair seats the same height, even if you must add a cushion to correct the difference.

❀ Create a color scheme for each meal. Select place mats, a tablecloth, or napkins that get your imagination going.

❀ When buying dinner plates, never buy more than eight that match. Any additional plates can be mixed with another set of plates. Most of your plates will look attractive together because you like them all; there will be connections of colors or patterns that link nicely.

❀ Linen bathroom hand towels make wonderful napkins and are less expensive to buy than table linens. Kitchen towels make great napkins for a French country bistro look; they're inexpensive and come in a large variety of cheerful patterns and colors.

❀ Napkin rings are festive. You can find them in housewares stores or at flea markets. They need not match— collect those that catch your fancy and your guests will relish them as much as you do.

❀ When dining with your spouse, put a potted plant or bowl of fruit at either end of the table to make it feel cozier.

❀ Once your children or grandchildren are old enough, let them help you set the table.

❀ If you have copper pots and casserole dishes, bringing them from oven or stove to table feels homey. Our favorite chef serves soup at the table from a copper soup pot.

❦ For a fun change, serve an oriental meal with chopsticks. You can buy colorful ones at museum gift stores as well as housewares stores.

❦ If you have some pretty porcelain tureens, you can use them as a centerpiece or for soup or dessert.

❦ Setting a table with place plates makes it look welcoming before you sit down. Any large dinner plates are fine.

❦ Set the table ahead of time. It whets your appetite for a fun experience and makes you party-ready.

As in all things beautiful there is an ideal.

WILLIAM JAMES

clothes: day and night

Clothes have a profound effect on our mood and spirit. When we select our clothes with care and an eye to enriching our personal sense of style, what we choose to wear is an enhancement of every day. The opportunity is there for each of us to do this, whether we shop in boutiques or browse in thrift shops. Paying attention to how we dress is an immediate, practical way to choose to increase our happiness.

On a scale from 1 to 10, how conscious are you about the way you dress to increase your happiness? How much attention do you pay to your wardrobe? Would you consider yourself fashion conscious? When you go shopping for clothes, do you like someone to shop with you to advise you? Has your taste in clothing changed dramatically over the years? What is your favorite season for clothes? Do you prefer

I'm sure you agree, that beauty is the only thing worth living for.

AGATHA CHRISTIE

casual sports clothes or do you love to get dressed up in black tie?

Go into your closet or dressing room. Look at all your clothes. Do you think your clothes represent your taste and ideal style? Do you enjoy thinking ahead about an event and planning what you want to wear? One of the biggest differences between men and women is that when a woman is asked to a wedding, the first thing she thinks about is what she is going to wear. Most men simply select a dark suit, a clean shirt, and, at the last minute, a necktie and a handkerchief. Women have far greater freedom in the way they dress than most men. The kind of work we do can restrict our dress preferences, but generally, women can use clothes to cheer themselves up, while expressing themselves and giving pleasure to others.

We are shaped and fashioned by what we love.

GOETHE

The way we decorate, the way we dress, and the way we live are intimately connected. I'm aware of what makes me feel comfortable in a room as well as of what clothes make me feel good about myself. Clothes are an opportunity for us to select from a variety of options, experimenting with different color combinations that will enhance our experience. I dress for my own happiness. I feel happiest wearing brightly colored clothes that are both fitted and stylish. Exotic color combinations bring me great joy.

wearing black

Most women love to wear black, particularly in cities. Black makes us feel sensuous and sexy. Black makes us look thinner than light colors. When I wear a black velvet or silk tunic top, I might choose to wear red satin slacks with black and red flats. I always wear color to contrast against black, even if it is just the piping along the edge of a jacket or a pink blouse that matches the lining of a jacket. I always wear color, even if no one sees it—the lining of black slacks could be bright acid green. I do this for me because it makes me happy.

> *The true meaning of life is to plant trees, under whose shade you do not expect to sit.*
>
> NELSON HENDERSON

Black looks great with white. When I wear black and white together, I think of the act in the classic musical *My Fair Lady* in which all the actors wear elegant black and white costumes. Besides red and fuchsia, turquoise, chartreuse, and acid green also look wonderful with black. Enjoy adding some color to your basic black.

scarves

I love my collection of scarves because they have fun patterns with vibrant color combinations. I have a silk scarf patterned in black, white, pink, and red. If I wear a pink blouse with a red blazer, the scarf around my neck lets the eye coordinate the color scheme. I love red and purple together, but most people would think this combination clashes. By wearing a scarf with lots of red and purple, I can make the combination more harmonious. My scarves encourage me to wear more daring color combinations.

> *Love consists in this, that two solitudes protect and touch and greet each other.*
>
> RAINER MARIA RILKE

please yourself

Choose to put on clothes that enhance your personal sense of well-being and joie de vivre. If it is dreary outside, I wear yellow, the psychological color of happiness.

For several years, Peter had a prejudice against any shade of green in clothing. He wasn't subtle about his lack of enthusiasm. In my inimitable way I continued to wear green, a favorite color, and, after all these years, he not only compliments me when I wear green but asks me to wear it at special times in our lives. I enjoy genuine compliments on my colorful clothes, but I try not to dress with the expectation of praise. Approximately 20 percent of my wardrobe is acid green. If I feel attractive wearing it, I radiate my feelings; they show in the way I carry myself and in my smile. Even if someone I love doesn't like what I wear, there is still an affectionate regard on their part for my sense of pleasure in my self-expression.

I am a part of all that I have met.

ALFRED, LORD TENNYSON

playful clothes

There are many opportunities in our day-to-day life for wearing more playful, colorful clothes. Take advantage of the clothes you wear by having fun. Think of your clothes as costumes. Build a wardrobe based on where and how you live, what you do each day, and what suits your per-

For everything that lives is holy, life delights in life.

WILLIAM BLAKE

sonality. Depending on your mood, as well as the occasion or season, dress in a more playful way. One of my favorite costumes is purple slacks, a fuchsia blouse, and an acid-green jacket with a scarf in precisely these three colors. When you feel playful inside, others often feel wonderful in your presence. When you are having fun, you encourage others to loosen up, and express their individuality more colorfully. We can mindfully dare to be ourselves. Only when we are courageous enough to break free from conservative, neutral colors and styling will we feel the freedom of being true to our inner twinkle.

> *Pleasure in moderation relaxes and tempers the spirit.*
>
> SENECA

intimate clothing

We can dress to express our spirit. There is more to underwear than pure practicality. There's a place for elegance, luxury, and style. We want to pamper ourselves, have some color as well as pattern. I enjoy indulging in lace bras in different colors that relate to what I'm wearing. A new pair of panties makes me feel good. Peter enjoys laying out his colorful boxer shorts along with his shirt, tie, and socks. Many of the patterns are the same as those of his pajamas or bathrobe. They're all refreshing to the senses.

> *He is the happiest, be he king or peasant, who finds peace in his home.*
>
> GOETHE

knock my socks off

Socks are important for comfort and ease as well as looks. I love colored tights and socks. They are accessories I appreciate, and I make an effort to add colors to my collection that will complement my wardrobe.

If you love everything, you will perceive the divine mystery in things.

DOSTOYEVSKY

Men can have some fun wearing colored socks on vacations and on weekends. I'm glad to see wonderful colors in men's socks at the store. There is so little color in a man's wardrobe that adding some socks in colors other than black, gray, brown, or navy blue is encouraging. When I wear colorful stockings or socks it makes me feel more bouncy. I'm mindful of how much fun colorful stockings and socks are. They make me feel young.

behind closed doors

Having attractive pajamas, nightgowns, and bathrobes make us feel wonderfully comfortable while in the privacy of our own home. I enjoy having some sensuous, soft "at home" outfits that would be inappropriate to wear out of doors. When we treat ourselves to nice things to wear to bed or for leisurely lounging around the house, we realize how much ease and pleasure these things bring to us day to day. When Peter wears pajamas and bathrobes that he likes, I appreciate seeing how attractive he looks. With dressing, as so many other areas, what we do for ourselves we do also for others.

happy colors

The colors we expose ourselves to in our physical environment echo our heart. By surrounding ourselves, our families, and friends with uplifting, delicious colors, colors fresh enough to eat, we increase everyone's happiness. Are you a colorist? Do you dream in vivid colors? Do you think in color, and are you sensitive to the different energies in all colors?

For without the private world of retreat one becomes virtually an unbalanced creature.

ELEANOR MCMILLEN

BROWN

We're all happier when the sky is blue, the sun is shining, the water is turquoise, and the grass is green. The colors that we instinctively find most life-enhancing and most charming are those we experience in nature—the cheerful colors of fruit, vegetables, flowering trees, and blossoming plants all make us feel wonderful.

pure and simple

Clear colors help us clarify our minds. Look at and learn from the colors of a rainbow. Red, orange, yellow, green, blue, and violet carry the pure vital energy that sustains nature and human nature. Breathe in the vital energy of refreshing colors; visualize yourself on a vacation on a sunny tropical island. Awaken to your deep-rooted connection to the wavelengths of energy in the colorful prism of light. I'm extremely fond of clear, soft, luminous pastels and fresh primary colors inspired by the clarity of a rainbow.

People could become happier if they brought more cheerful colors into their immediate lives. Living a colorful life makes us forever young. Perhaps it is time to reevaluate your color palette, to get in touch with an inner garden in bloom and open your heart to the colors that make you smile. In some areas of our lives we're forced to compromise; money is a consideration, yet color is an exception. Items in happy colors cost the same amount of money as those in drab shades that drain our energy. Because color is the quickest, easiest, and least expensive form of self-expression, explore ways to be true to the pure, clear beauty of your favorite colors.

It is neither wealth nor splendor, but tranquility and occupation which give happiness.

THOMAS JEFFERSON

We are sensitive to the effects of color on our mood and energy whether we are aware of it or not. By studying the different colors we are drawn to, by looking at the color combinations we love, we will learn how to use colors to heal us, soothe us, and uplift us. As we train our eyes to look and really see the subtle differences in tints of red, orange, yellow, green, blue, and violet, we can find ways to bring these colors close to us.

Focus your attention on the colors that make you feel bouncy, that give you great pleasure. Before you recycle or give away your magazines, go through each page to see what colors catch your eye and stimulate you. Look at an ad; look at pictures of gardens and room interiors. Cut out colors you like and clip or glue them in a notebook. Go to a local paint store and select eight or ten paint chips you like. Don't concern yourself with where they may end up. Buy a quart or two of paint you like on your paint chips. Throw in a few disposable paintbrushes.

It is right to celebrate.

SAINT LUKE

Once home, find a place for one of your colors. Have some fun with this. You might want to paint a towel rack in the bathroom a heavenly blue; the chartreuse could end up inside your kitchen drawers. A serene peach could cheer up the inside of your white wicker wastebasket. A sunny yellow could land on a closet ceiling.

identify your happy colors

All colors have associations. Consider the colors you're drawn to—the lilac you paint on your bathroom walls may remind you of the lilac tree outside your childhood bedroom window, or the robin's egg blue may remind you of watching the eggs in a nest as a young child, until they hatched into chicks. If you have this association, you would never want to throw away a Tiffany box or shopping bag, because the Tiffany blue is a symbol of happy hatchings.

> *Joy is a revelation of what was unknown before.*
>
> ROLLO MAY

We can express our happiness through color because it often speaks louder and more brilliantly than words. When I graduated from junior high school, I donated purple iris and hot pink peonies from our garden to decorate the auditorium. Not only do I hold these flowers dear but the colors bring back this nostalgic memory.

By paying careful attention to every color you choose, you will see your authentic color palette emerge. If you want to change your colors from neutral tones to brighter, cleaner, clearer tints, start editing out the items that are no longer exciting and cheerful. Choose a bright-colored coat the next time you buy one. Wear a wildly bright silk scarf around your neck or in a blazer pocket and smile back as people smile at you. You will feel happier right away. So will the observer.

Pay attention to the color of the stationery box as well as that of the paper and the lining of the envelope. The color of your watch strap is something you see hundreds of times a day. The color of the pen you use to write with and the color of the ink are your choice. Everything in your physical environment can be of a chosen color if you are alert to the powerful hold color has on your psyche.

The next time you go shopping for a raincoat, try on a yellow or red one rather than beige. Look at every possession you have and dream of its being more vibrant, more lively, or just more fun. Whether buying eyeglasses or candles, suitcases, tote bags, purses, wallets, notebooks, stamps, stockings, storage boxes, tape measures, mailing envelopes, socks, notepaper, pens, ink, bathrobes, pajamas, napkins, hand towels and bathing suits, express your playful, enthusiastic self in all your clothes, accessories, and gear. When we brighten up, we lighten up.

Joy helps you to be with people in a way that sparks your energy and leaves you fulfilled.

CHARLOTTE DAVIS

KASL

Open your eyes wide to each pretty color you experience. Notice how pleasing some color combinations are and how they make you feel. If you love wearing a lilac bathrobe lined in lemon yellow, try putting yellow towels in the bathroom you just painted. Play until you feel the colors sing. Any color that makes you feel good you can wear. If you feel great wearing red, red will look attractive on you.

colorful living

A colorful life greatly increases our happiness. As the stark palette of winter gives way to the vibrant hues of spring, the dull and drab colors in our lives, if you redecorate, can turn into luminescent fresh colors and transform our spirits. I visualize this rebirth in nature as the cycle comes around in April, renewing our faith in life's eternal promise to bud and blossom, sprout new life, bring refreshing energy around us and inside us.

there's happiness here

Right here, in the midst of our daily lives, we experience happiness when we remain mindful of all the little rituals we can create and perform throughout the day and evening. I have a small bell on my desk that I ring from time to time to remind myself to stay focused on right now, right here.

We are uplifted when we deliberately notice the smallest details, the things that make us feel good, the pretty items we love. We choose a cup and saucer for tea that suits our current mood. Looking at the hand-painted lily-of-the-valley decoration on a favorite cup reminds me of our wedding in May, when the girls and I carried bouquets of this delicate fragrant flower that looks like tiny white bells. This nostalgia, along with the visualization of that happy day, greatly enhances my tea ritual. I can feel the reverberation of the church bells that clanged in celebration after the wedding.

When love and skill work together, expect a masterpiece.

JOHN RUSKIN

Sitting at your writing table with a candle and some flowers, some favorite photographs, a colorful painting above you, taking time to write in your journal or to write a letter to a child—there is happiness here. Meditate for a moment on the fact that our immediate happiness is all we will ever have. These fleeting seconds when we're awake, fully alive to the magic of these simple moments spontaneously lived, accumulate and build, giving us the foundation for living a happy life.

It is not doing the thing we like to do, but liking the thing we have to do that makes life blessed.

GOETHE

surprises

Living, breathing moments are opportunities to find the happiness you seek. The smallest things can bring you great joy when you love them. What surprises will this moment bring to you? What delight will come to you out of the blue? Reading a book that inspires you and gives you insights, receiving a package in the mail from a friend who thought of you when she saw the blue and white cocktail napkins and wrapped them in pretty paper and ribbon, with a sweet note.

timing

Waiting to do the dishes until the sun swings around to the window in front of the kitchen sink makes me nod and say, ah, yes, this is the time of day when the dishes will be done with ease and pleasure. Going out for a walk in a snowstorm, wearing a comfortable pair of shoes, looking through a collection of art post-cards you've collected over dozens of years, walking into a room when your spouse looks up and smiles and tells you how pretty you look or simply says, "I love you." There's happiness here.

On a beautiful warm spring day, taking the children to the beach, playing in the sand, swimming, running along the water's edge together, gathering seashells; there's happiness here. Planning a family vacation to the lake, going to the doctor's office with a small child for a checkup, having a mother-daughter lunch together after the appointment, then going to the shoe store to buy some new red shoes and yellow boots for your five-year-old grandchild. There's happiness here.

Sitting at the kitchen table, lingering after breakfast, reading the paper with your lover, doing errands together because you adore each other, telling jokes at the post office to make the line appear to go faster, sitting on a bench in the park under a flowering apple tree surrounded by daffodils and listening to the birds singing their hearts out; there's happiness here.

> *Live in each season as it passes; and resign yourself to the influences of each.*
>
> HENRY DAVID
>
> THOREAU

Folding the laundry, smelling the freshness, putting clean clothes in the drawers is satisfying. Emptying the bags of groceries and putting the fresh food in the refrigerator as we anticipate delicious meals is a ritual that makes us feel good. Arranging a platter of fruit adds aesthetic delight. Receiving tickets in the mail for a trip you're taking with your family gives you a lift on a busy day.

The hand towels we put out for guests, the fresh bar of almond soap, the flowers we arrange in a pitcher, the snack we prepare ahead of time for our children and their friends after school; these gestures encourage our sense of anticipation by sweetening our moments with pleasant thoughts of loved ones.

having a love affair with life

When we're happy, we're living the life we're meant to live. We're being true to our inner nature, to who we really are. Our profound love of life is powerfully sustaining. Creating paradise on earth is having a love affair with life. Each hour, we can bring nearer to us more beauty, more loveliness, more things we value: a richer understanding of the reality of cause and effect, a growing library of good literature, a collection of life-enhancing paintings and drawings by favorite artists, an increasing knowledge about what ingredients go into a happy moment, a deeper appreciation for every breath of air we inhale and gratitude at being alive.

What we have loved others will love, and we will teach them how.

WILLIAM

WORDSWORTH

the breath of life

Our life is a creative process, not a destination. We will never arrive at a time or a place; our paradise is lived now, as we breathe in and breathe out. We can't hold our breath for long. Each moment is ours to live; each experience is an opportunity to learn, to grow, to improve, and to love.

In his first inaugural address in 1933, Franklin Delano

Roosevelt said to an unhappy nation, "Happiness lies not in the mere possession of money; it lies in the joy of achievement, in the thrill of creative effort." Our greatest accomplishment on this earthly journey is to be well along the path toward greater happiness. In our daily lives, when we find pleasure in what we choose to do, we will know happiness firsthand. Raising children, growing a garden, decorating a room, telling a story, planning dinner, or organizing a fundraiser, we experience the "thrill of creative effort," mindful of the gift of life day by day. Wherever, whenever you love, there is happiness, and paradise is your earthly home.

The skies can't keep their secret!
They tell it to the hills—
the hills just tell the
orchards—and they
the daffodils.

EMILY DICKINSON

dreams come true

Love is an attempt to change a piece of the dream-world into reality.

—THEODORE REIK

Dare to live the life you have dreamed for yourself. Go forward and make your dreams come true.

—EMERSON

the pursuit of life

In Tolstoy's wise short story entitled "The Emperor's Three Questions," the questions posed were: What is the best time to do each thing? Who are the most important people to work with? and, What is the most important thing to do at all times?

Whoever answered all three questions would win a great prize. The emperor ended up at a wise old hermit's hut on a mountain top, where the hermit was sowing seeds. The hermit's answers were: "Remember that there is only one important time and that is now. The present moment is the only time over which we have dominion. The most important person is the one you are with, who is right before you, for who knows if you will have dealings with any other person in the future. The most important pursuit is making the person standing at your side happy, for that alone is the pursuit of life."

Some men see things as they are and say "Why?" I dream of things that never were and say, "Why not?"

ROBERT FROST

It is good advice for all of us to consciously contemplate being sensitive to the person next to us, who will always need a handshake, a kind word, or a simple caring gesture. "Life, liberty and the pursuit of happiness" is our birthright and privilege. The way we pursue happiness is to generate it and spread it wherever we are, whoever we are with right now.

dream big dreams

Be idealistic. No one on earth deserves to be happier than you do. Because you are unique, if you are not happy, no one can be happy for you. Happiness is love in action. The more you love your life, the more you will love all of life. You can accomplish great things when your energy is loving. It is recognizing what we love inside and out that leads us to greater happiness.

Live the life you've imagined.

HENRY DAVID

THOREAU

What do you want to send out into the

universe? What are some of your big dreams? How many of your dreams have already come true? What is your vision for the rest of your life? Dreams come true when there is a clear, far-sighted perspective on what we most want from life and what energies we are willing to expend to achieve it. When we dream of a better life, we can work hard to succeed in creating one. We can't do everything in one brief lifetime, but we can do some things really well, things that are deeply satisfying and meaningful to us as well as useful to others.

Always dream and shoot higher than you know you can do.

WILLIAM FAULKNER

You can do what you love the most. This requires your courage in inventing what you are most excited about doing. What makes you happy most likely will also be a worthwhile contribution to the world. Keep this in your mind and heart as you deliberately focus on following through with your passionate interests.

what makes people happy?

Rushing robs us of our ability to be fully conscious of each experience. Being obsessive planners, constantly attacking our "to do" list and being controlling about the outcome, blinds us to intelligent appreciation of the potential joy right here, right now.

All of us live out what we really think and feel deep down inside.

ROBERT SCHULLER

Kennon M. Sheldon, a professor of psychology at the University of Missouri, conducted a study to answer the elusive question, "What makes people happy?" He found that people are happy when they are doing things

they freely choose, that express who they are, that they do rea-
sonably well, that give them a sense of connectedness to others
and make them feel good about themselves.
He believes that a lot of good moments add up
to a good life. Good moments, he says, are
made up of "feeling that your activities are self-
chosen and self-endorsed, feeling that you are
effective in your activities, feeling a sense of
closeness to others, and self-esteem." He
believes that we should try to do as many things as we can that we
feel an internal attraction to, explore our talents and interests,
and try to pick things that we have some natural ability for.

> *Dreams are the touchstones of our character.*
>
> HENRY DAVID THOREAU

internal attractions

Try to feel a personal connection to whatever you experience.
You can read a book, feeling the words were written just for you.
We may also feel this connection with art or
music, or when we eat a chef's perfectly prepared meal—we feel one with the experience.
Excellent moments of pleasure are within our
reach throughout the day. No one sustains
intense happiness all the time, but heightened moments add up
to a life well lived and appreciated.

> *I don't believe in failure.*
>
> OPRAH WINFREY

As you listen to a favorite piece of classical music, look for
the phrases that move you the most. Perhaps you can buy more
CDs of Beethoven's symphonies. If you're sipping a cup of
espresso at Starbucks, perhaps you have a fantasy of putting an
espresso machine on your wish list in order to make your own

heavenly coffee at home and share it with friends in the warm atmosphere you've created. If you always feel happy when you dance in the arms of your lover, make it a priority to share a dance whenever you can, even if you spontaneously dance to some favorite music at home just for the fun of moving to the rhythm. These opportunities are within our control. We can choose the quality of our moments by following our hearts.

> *We must be willing to get rid of the life we've planned, so as to have the life that is waiting for us.*
>
> JOSEPH CAMPBELL

be happy

Society traditionally has not encouraged us to be introspective, to look into our own thoughts, feelings and sensations. I believe self-examination should become a daily habit. Many people do amazing and heroic things with their lives. We can too. When we make time and space for inner work, we can improve our sense of caring for others and ourselves, becoming kinder, more compassionate, and more loving.

We're most effective when we're enjoying what we're doing. Our passionate interest in whatever we do is contagious. When we concentrate on taking care of our immediate needs as well as our future goals, we create a more harmonious balance between giving to others and receiving life's bounties. We have a large capacity to change our life for the better, to inwardly transform ourselves. We can be agents of amazing change. The life you are leading now doesn't have to stay the same. By remaining open and

> *Voyage, travel, and change of place impart vigor.*
>
> SENECA

honest, you can see with greater clarity what minor and major changes you are free to choose that will bring greater happiness. Our goal should be to use our energy in the most positive ways possible to increase our own happiness as well as to enhance the greater well-being of others.

Choose well.

HOMER

The lens you habitually look through may not be the clearest one available. We don't need to go through life with the desperate feeling that "this isn't it." We can dream big dreams and have wonderful things happen to us. Sometimes it is necessary to use our own inner searchlight to explore our dreams and become more visionary. The greater our capacity to see what is tangible and physical as well as what is intangible and invisible, the more successfully we dream.

We don't have to leave our everyday environment to do our necessary inner work. Our inner world and our outer environment should be continuously informing each other, making the connections between our intuitive thoughts and our honest actions. Here, wherever we are, in the small, simple acts, in the choices we make to live up to our happier selves, we see how one thing leads to another.

There are only two roads that lead to something like human happiness. They are marked by the words: love and achievement.

THEODORE REIK

We feel able to direct and redirect our actions in affirming ways that lead us further on our path toward our dreams and goals.

change can be transforming

What are some habits you would like to change? We have to free ourselves up to have our dreams come true. Maybe you and a friend have been taking morning walks, but you now feel an urge to have more solitude in order to listen to your own voice. You want to continue to see your friend but want to break the habit of meeting each morning, because you need this time for contemplation. This one small change of habit can make a world of difference if you use your time alone wisely. We need regular times alone to better understand what is happening inside us and around us and to integrate our lives into a larger perspective.

We are our choices.

JEAN-PAUL SARTRE

the power of purpose

Set some clear goals for yourself, focusing on keeping as many of your options open as possible. Because happiness is always now, and always a journey, to be happier we should enjoy it. A moment fully savored and appreciated leads us toward a happy life. Our lives are made up of thousands of little thoughts, choices and steps we take every day. We can link them together to make them a brilliant reflection of our dreams, our highest aspirations.

As we move forward in a systematic way, we see good results of our efforts. Even when our intentions are honorable, there may still be obstacles in our way. Yet whenever we give our life our best, we will seldom live with regrets. When we take care of the little things, there is a sense of order, of satisfaction that we are doing our best to improve our immediate lives. There are no external forces that can keep us from staying in touch with what we value. Our inner work will show us what we need to do to make positive changes in our outer world.

inner questioning brings clarity

There will never be any question about your own happiness that you won't be able to answer for yourself if you are willing to be introspective, to closely examine the core of your true nature. What do you feel you need more of in your life right now? Do you think you need to make more time to be with your children? Do you also feel a need to make more uninterrupted time to contemplate, study, and meditate, to closely inspect your inner world?

> *I believe four ingredients are necessary for happiness: health, warm personal relations, sufficient means to keep you from want, and successful work.*
>
> BERTRAND RUSSELL

Are there some things you want more of? Perhaps your apartment is too small and you feel confined; your energy is blocked. Or maybe you need more sunlight in order to feel more cheerful day to day. You could find that you are working too hard being "success-ful," earning money but not feeling that what you are doing is meaningful.

Are you living the life of your dreams? Right now, can you identify some areas of concern so that you can take concrete steps to improve your present situation? Knowing this moment

Knowledge of what is possible is the beginning of happiness.

GEORGE SANTAYANA

will never come again, we must live life well and deeply, now or never. The time to dream big dreams is now. We can't afford to procrastinate, putting our lives on hold. It is later than you think.

no one to blame

We can identify specific things to do that will make us happier and then take action. When we become clear about what we want, we can consciously make time for what's more important to us. I remember several years ago telling one of my daughters that I hadn't given myself enough time to read and write. She immediately told me I had no one to blame but myself. Often others who love us see more clearly what we struggle with inwardly.

pictures of hope

Our dreams are detailed pictures of what we ardently wish for. We look forward to something we desire and expect will work out. Let yourself dream. By projecting positive wishes, and hoping to have them realized, you have started the process that leads you to the results you most want. Pay attention to your visualization. When you put your energy in the direction of what you hope, you will propel your dreams toward realization.

I wish you all the joy that you can wish.

SHAKESPEARE

A young married couple made a lot of money in their jobs in the Wall Street invest-

ment world. Together they dreamed of leasing out their apartment for a year and traveling around the world. They had
enough money saved. They had no children.
Only their own limited vision could keep them
from dreaming this big dream and having it
work out. They both wanted to quit the rat
race of the stock market and take jobs teaching
at a university after their exciting adventure.
They had enthusiastic support from family
and friends who joined them for visits in
exotic places. This trip was a big dream that
came true because they didn't allow anything
to hold them back.

> *The secret of joy in work is contained in one word: excellence. To know how to do something well is to enjoy it.*
>
> ANATOLE BROYARD

My aunt Betty certainly was full of hope when she dreamed
of taking her three oldest nieces around the world. And now,
having been taken on the trip, I feel comfortable traveling anywhere and everywhere, ready for the incredible thrill of experiencing different cultures, meeting interesting people, feeling
the exhilaration of broadening my horizons, and gaining a
deeper perspective. Now might be the time to dream impossible dreams and, with confident expectation, see how well things
work out. Plan now for your new exciting adventure.

be the change you want to see

Once you have a vision of what might be possible, then fear-
lessly believe in yourself to make your dreams come true. Have
faith in yourself. A writer friend is figuring out the story for
her next novel. Every day she walks to work alone, letting the

It's a funny thing about life; if you refuse to accept anything but the best, you very often get it.

WILLIAM SOMERSET

MAUGHAM

characters take shape. She goes to a coffee shop next to the office to take notes before she loses the muse. Following your dream takes enormous courage because you are not going along with what is already out there; you are charting new territory. As Gandhi taught us, "Be the change you want to see in the world."

Our dreams are always ours alone. Others have their own unique dreams. It is vital to keep your dreams alive. Work toward your goals each day. You are the one messenger. Without you, many useful and exciting things will never exist.

a healthy baby

A friend got pregnant in her early forties and after three months went into labor. Her labor was successfully delayed, following a short hospital stay, and she dreamed of doing whatever it took to have a healthy child. For six months she was bedridden, many of the months hospitalized. What a small price to pay in the big picture of life for the privilege of giving birth, full-term, to a healthy son. She had the vision of doing whatever was necessary to carry her child to term. It was her vision of her long-range goal that sustained her during her confinement. Dreams come true, but not without sacrifice and commitment.

Fortune sides with those who dare.

VIRGIL

dreaming your dreams

Timing is central to our lasting happiness. What is right for us at one point in our life may not be significant at another. Be sure your dreams are authentic expressions of your inner world. If you dream of having a child, for example, this is a huge commitment that will forever change your life. It is one of the most serious choices you will ever make. Some people are not meant to be parents.

Other people would call it work. But I'm just playing very hard.

JACK LENOR LARSON

When you dream of becoming a parent, and want it with your whole heart, one way or another you'll figure out, in your circumstances, how to make it happen.

Keep dreaming your dreams until your divine inner intelligence says yes, and when you know for sure that something is right, follow your heart all the way through. Be open and receptive. Don't resist anything. Everything can work out. Trust yourself.

short-term, long-term happiness

Dreams are different from goals. If you dream of a happier life with a specific vision of how to accomplish it, you're able to set certain goals as strategies for making your dreams a reality. Dreams come true more effectively when you try to realize them through meeting short-term and long-term goals. Examine the two levels of your

Just one great idea can completely revolutionize your life.

EARL NIGHTENGALE

My share of the work of the world may be limited, but the fact that it is work makes it precious.

HELEN KELLER

dreams. You have the long-range future—what would you like to be able to say as you look back on your life? You also have the here-and-now dream of how you want to feel at the end of today.

Each goal, like every dream, should bring you greater overall happiness in your immediate life. If you have an important paper to write, it will probably make you a lot happier to get a jump-start on the research rather than be anxious over the impending deadline and always feel the crunch. Many people claim they work best under pressure. This may or may not be true, but usually when we put pressure on ourselves, others also suffer. Is it going to make you happier to wait until the last minute, having had to endure the anguish of having a heavy responsibility hanging over you? It will be less arduous for you to do the paper now, instead of procrastinating. Borrow my "carrot theory" of looking forward to having a sensuous dinner with your partner after having completed the work.

The man who is born with a talent which he is meant to use finds his greatest happiness in using it.

GOETHE

Think of your short-term happiness—what you are experiencing instant-by-instant—as well as your long-term happiness. We don't want our lives to become one never-ending "to do" list where we continuously worry and plan for the unknown future. If you feel hesitation or uncertainty about what you should do now, ask yourself, "Is it going to make me happy if I get going on this task?" Keep focused on your goal to get yourself into a happier state of consciousness. The little task done now helps. You might choose to pay your bills before taking the children to the beach. You'll unburden your mind, have a clear conscience, and feel free to spend a carefree afternoon with your family.

If you do something you love, you can't help but be successful.

ELISABETH
KÜBLER-ROSS

If you've set a long-term goal to lose weight and you find yourself tempted by a piece of chocolate cake after dinner, ask yourself what is more important to you. What is going to make you happier: the immediate indulgence, or the sacrifice in favor of your long-range plan to slim down? There are times when we choose the short-term happiness with our eyes wide open. I was on a plane, reading, when a flight attendant handed me some nibbles with my Diet Coke. I was tired, thirsty, hungry, and feeling a bit naughty. Yes, I ate the salty snack, licking my fingers. Whatever this indulgence cost me was worth it. What's important is not to let our short-term happiness cloud our vision of the long-term goals that will help us realize our dreams. On the other hand, our long-term happiness should not take away the joy of the day-to-day pleasures that sustain us. There must be some balance to our life.

big dream, bigger house

If you truly want a bigger house with a fenced yard, you can save your money each week toward this goal. When you put your good energy out there, good things will come to you. Be patient with yourself as you take small steps toward big dreams. You will find your ideal house when you are focused on what you want. Keep an open mind about what the actual house will

Well done is better than well said.

BENJAMIN FRANKLIN

look like. How you feel is far more important than appearances.

By thinking thoughts that inspire your best actions, you'll be willing to make necessary sacrifices that will allow your dream to come true. When you and your spouse are willing to buy a wreck of a house that has good bones and fix it up yourselves, you'll be happy to do so, because you'll have more space for your growing family. The hard work that you both put into the house brings you closer and gives you a greater appreciation of living in a house that you love.

We work to become, not to acquire.

ELBERT HUBBARD

taking action now

A dream without action is only a fantasy. A dream becomes your reality when you follow through with the necessary action. If you sincerely want to be a writer, painter, or doctor, you must build your life around this dream, working diligently every day toward what you believe will bring you great happiness throughout your life.

Take small actions every day to move your dreams forward. Whatever you want to do with your life, do it now. Whatever good you visualize, begin it now. There will never be a better time than the reality of right now. Write down some of your yearnings, your burning desires. Visualize the steps you will take to reach your goal. Everything you do with passion and love will lead you in the direction of fulfilling big dreams.

All happiness depends on courage and work.

HONORÉ DE BALZAC

A friend was a kitchen designer for years. One day she was

seated at the drafting table creating a plan for a client, envisioning the best location for the appliances, when she suddenly
visualized herself opening up a tea and coffee
house in a New England village; a cozy place
that could become a meeting house for the
local people and summer tourists. She and
her husband chose Stonington Village, where
she found an old yellow house, and she named
her shop *The Yellow House*. Recently she told Peter and me over
dinner that her intuitive feeling had led her in pursuit of her
dream until it was born and alive. Mary Ellen loves her life. Her
realized dream is a central part of her happiness.

> *Every calling is great
> when greatly pursued.*
>
> OLIVER WENDELL
>
> HOLMES, JR.

say yes

Mary Ellen listened, paid attention, and acted on her dream. If
you have a similar urge to own your own business, what concrete
steps can you take today to work toward your goal? You can
research what is involved. You can save money while you are still
on a salary, because it is shocking to become the
boss who now has a payroll! You can look into
health insurance rates as well as office rents.

Many people are afraid to take the initial
steps toward their ideal life because they fear
failure. When we sincerely try our best, we seldom fail. We learn from our mistakes and
wisely don't make the same one twice. When
our goal is to succeed, our energy is used constructively and we
look for ways to work out solutions.

> *What the mind cries
> out for is serious
> work . . . that a
> living spirit must have
> or perish.*
>
> MICHAEL DRURY

making plans

Every man loves what he is good at.

THOMAS SHADWELL

We would drift through life if we didn't make plans and stick with them, but having a plan should not make us rigid. On the contrary, planning contributes to our sense of possibility in making our dreams come true. Planning arranges our life in an intelligent pattern. Only we know how much time to plan for various projects, or how much time to plan for being alone. No matter how much we love others, there will be times we'll want to push the world aside in order to be free to do what we need to do, what we know in our hearts is right for us.

say no

The Glorious Impossibilities . . . bring joy to our hearts, hope to our lives, songs to our lips.

MADELEINE L'ENGLE

What happens when someone asks you to do something with them on an evening you'd planned to stay home to be quiet and cozy, to catch up on your reading? When you choose what you feel is the right balance for you, often you will turn down invitations or requests from others. Saying you're not able to do something, or that you have a conflict, or simply that it is not a good time, is sincere. Train yourself daily to say no nicely and firmly.

If you plan to have an intimate weekend alone with your husband, it is hardly appropriate to agree to a friend's last-minute visit to your small house. When you plan to spend a weekend doing home repairs and some gardening, it is not a good time to entertain an old college friend who asks to stay with you the day before. Even if someone is willing to stay at a nearby bed-and-breakfast, if you and your family already have made plans, you may choose not to dilute this special family time.

The reason a lot of people do not recognize opportunity is because it usually goes around wearing overalls looking like hard work.

THOMAS EDISON

No is a wonderful word. When you're caring and kind as you say it, everyone maintains dignity. You are not being insensitive by saying no when it is appropriate. Joy comes from a disciplined, well-ordered life, not one where we say yes to everything that comes our way. The grace in our life may be in what we don't do because it gives us freedom to do what we choose to do without noise, distraction, and interference.

I have enormous respect for people's privacy because I value my own so highly. When we are alone, we don't have to answer to anyone but our conscience. These private hours when we create time and space for quiet contemplation give us such richness. We're able to freely flow into work and projects with no conflicting obligations to others. If I ask a grandchild to come for supper and am told that it isn't a good night because of a biology exam the next morning, I understand completely. As adults we need to value our own and others' projects, plans, or deadlines that bring meaning and satisfaction to life.

Is not this the true romantic feeling—not to desire to escape life, but to prevent life from escaping you.

THOMAS WOLFE

Making plans regularly to do what needs to be done as well as what we choose to accomplish focuses our energies on our goals and dreams. When we're caring in our planning, we don't have to let our family or ourselves down. We'll have plenty of time to see our friends when it is mutually good timing.

a strong heart

Courage is often accompanied by natural fear. We are all afraid of the darkness of the unknown; we tend to fear change. But unless we choose to make significant changes in our lives to make things better, there is no possibility of our dreams coming true. Maybe your dream is to become a designer, or you want to become a motivational speaker, or you decide your calling is to become a holistic healer. Whenever you choose change over permanency, when you are aiming to improve your life, you will always have the necessary strength even if you also feel fear. Your brave heart is there, waiting to be put to good use.

When you work you fulfill a part of earth's furthest dream.

KAHLIL GIBRAN

Dwell on visualizing your dream. All things are sweetened by risk. We experience physiological and psychological well-being when we pay attention to our happier nature. The only way we can improve our lives is by accepting inevitable changes that lift us up to greater well-being and fulfillment. If we resist change we get stuck. When we're resilient, willing to explore, to look forward to a new adventure, we can use our curiosity and look forward to the wonder and mystery inherent in small events and fleeting moments.

serendipity connects us to our dreams

Being rather than doing allows us to be fully receptive to the joy of each moment. When we let serendipity enhance our experiences, we live with a far greater sense of pleasure. Be on the lookout for the gift of making fortunate discoveries by accident. A great deal of happiness comes as a result of the things we are not consciously searching for but discover with surprise. We can delight in the reality of any given moment. There are many different ways we become stimulated by the discovery of something totally unexpected, surprising, and beneficial.

Profound joy of the heart is like a magnet that indicates the path of life. One has to follow it, even though one enters into a way full of difficulties.

MOTHER TERESA

When Peter and I were looking for a house to buy in southeastern Connecticut, preferably in the village of Stonington, we drove down Water Street there, thinking we were looking for a parking place. We parked in front of a house with a plaque that read REVEREND JOHN RATHBONE, CIRCA 1775. Next to the plaque was a sign—FOR SALE. Parking in front of this house was indeed serendipitous. We found our house before we ever started serious house hunting.

We planned a romantic trip to Paris for our twenty-sixth wedding anniversary in May and discovered that our favorite artist Roger Mühl was having a major exhibition in Paris at the same time. We all are blessed with these wonderful happenings. I was playing in the

One can live magnificently in this world, if one knows how to work and how to love.

LEO TOLSTOY

> *If one advances confidently in the direction of his dreams, he will meet with a success unexpected in common hours.*
>
> HENRY DAVID
> THOREAU

women's doubles finals tennis tournament at a club in Connecticut with Peter's sister as my partner. Peter came to cheer her on to win the silver cup, and I ended up marrying my tennis partner's baby brother twenty years later.

Being open and receptive to all of life's serendipitous occurrences brings us great happiness. These surprises, these mysterious occurrences, are "meant to be." Appreciate them. Don't wait to understand the mystery before embracing the moment. Don't wait to become wise in hindsight. Try to see with 20/20 vision now.

life's defining moments

Voltaire understood that "Paradise is where I am." Wherever we go, we carry the universe within us, feeling deeply connected to everything. As Constantine Catafy reminds us, "No ship will ever take you away from yourself." When we're open and receptive, living a sensuous life, we'll experience more moments that deeply define us.

> *Life is too short to neglect any opportunities.*
>
> BROOKE STODDARD

Think back on defining moments that have given form and meaning to your life. Take a few minutes to reflect and bring them into focus. One central determining moment of my life, as I've mentioned, was becoming suddenly conscious of beauty in my mother's flower garden when I was three. At fifteen, I took an art history course from an elderly artist-teacher, Phyl Gardner, who confirmed my intuition that I was meant to be earthy and more playfully creative. Just two years later, I met my mentor, Eleanor McMillen Brown, when she gave a lecture at the New York School of Interior Design. I knew I had to work for her design firm: Mrs. Brown was elegant, dignified, talented, and confident. When I was nineteen years old, I saw the paintings of a young French artist, Roger Mühl. As a result of my passion for his work, I enjoy helping clients to feel happier in their homes each day, living with his colorful creations.

Nothing is impossible to a willing heart.

JOHN HEYWOOD

As dreams come true, everything connects in visible as well as invisible ways. Because of my love of Mühl's paintings, within a year we met and became friends. Two years later, on our way to visit Roger and his wife, Line, in the South of France, there was a bad storm. We had to stop driving because the streets were flooded. We parked in front of an antiques store in the village where the Mühls lived at the time. We went in, and I fell in love with a beautifully carved marble-topped Regency fruitwood table. I've learned that there is no such thing as an inanimate object if you love it; this table powerfully spoke to me. Traveling on to Florence, I dreamed of this table night and day. Fortunately I listened to the signals; I called the antiques dealer from Italy and bought the table. This is one object of my affection I know for certain was meant for me to love and care for.

My candle burns at both ends; it will not last the night; but ah, my foes, and oh, my friends—it gives a lovely light.

EDNA ST. VINCENT MILLAY

I received my first big decorating commission when I was in my early twenties. I was given a newly built Georgian house in Connecticut to decorate from scratch; the client was the mother

> *It may be those who do most, dream most.*
>
> STEPHEN LEACOCK

of a dear friend. I was to be in charge, with Mrs. Brown looking over my shoulder. This was my big break. Not only was I able to advance in my career as an interior designer; as I worked on this project I gave birth to our first daughter, Alexandra, confirming my belief that I was born to be a mother.

We should try to be receptive to the positive clues we regularly receive and find ways to put them to constructive use. Defining moments are turning points, when we gain self-confidence in the experiences that contribute to our overall well-being, our sense of meaning in our lives, and our understanding that our dreams are coming true.

We will continue to have moments that shape and form our character, that nourish us on our journey. These transcendent moments give us fresh insights into greater wisdom.

perfect moments

Because happiness is always to be found wherever we are, the most ordinary time can become a magical moment. Walking in the snow, crunching along in high yellow boots, all snuggled in

> *I've learned that the person with big dreams is more powerful than the one with all the facts.*
>
> HENRY JACKSON, JR.

warm clothes, we're caught by surprise at how silent, how pure, and how beautiful the majestic trees look, as well as at the perfect pattern of a snowflake we may examine. When we go to our child's room to announce that dinner is ready, we can end up on the floor playing jacks or Legos or reading a favorite story. Dinner can wait. We know that holding a baby or walking in a beautiful garden or seeing a rainbow after rain or getting up to watch the sunrise will be moments of awe. We can deliberately try to expose ourself to these uplifting pleasurable experiences whenever possible.

Seek happiness in the present, and you'll find it in the future.

KAZUO SUZUKI

"ah"

When we practice present-moment mindfulness, we can fully appreciate a perfect moment. We say "ah," feeling that all's well with the world. When did you last experience a perfect moment? Can you identify several that stand out in the last week? Think of a perfect moment as a happiness spark, a timeless experience when you are fully alive, loving your intimate connection to whatever is happening. These perfect moments occur as we think, see, and feel with great clarity into the depths of our being.

A friend recognizes his perfect moments instantaneously. Charles is in touch with his thoughts, his senses, and his extrasensory powers. When everything falls into place ideally, he always smiles, gently exhales, saying almost under his breath, "ah," and then he taps the table where

May you live every day of your life.

JONATHAN SWIFT

he is seated with his hand twice as if to confirm, "This is the way life should be." This ritual comforts me as well. When we recognize extraordinary grace as it is revealed to us, appreciation of our happiness deepens. All experiences have the power to transform us when we're fully alive to the beauty of a present moment's encounter.

nothing will ever be the same

Some perfect moments are carefully planned, others mysteriously happen. Often they happen when we will something special to happen and then, as though by luck, it happens more beautifully than imagined or anticipated. These perfect moments are ephemeral, not automatic. When we try to re-create a perfect moment, we have high expectations that usually lead to disappointment. Each new vital experience has freshness, innocence, originality, and character.

Human happiness and human satisfaction must ultimately come from within oneself.

DALAI LAMA

Think of some of your most memorable, perfect moments. Visualize as many as you can. They need not be monumental. Your dog wags his tail at you and licks your face. This constitutes an ideal moment because you are both present for each other. Sometimes all it takes is being there. Timing is crucial to creating the right atmosphere for these perfect moments to bloom. We have to wait for the perfect ripeness before we savor cantaloupe or honeydew melon. The same is true of tomatoes or avocado. And of love.

If we put on some favorite music, then leave the room to make phone calls, we have distracted ourselves from being present and letting the music inspire us. If we oversleep and need to rush to get to work, all the important personal rituals we usually perform that create an abundance of perfect moments have been taken away, and we get off to an anxious start on our workday. Was staying up late worth the disruption of our morning rituals and disciplines?

Nothing has value except for the hunger one has for it.

CAMILLE COROT

making honey

Practice a single-object meditation. Focus your attention on an object, looking at it as if for the first time. Hold a picture frame and really look into a picture of yourself as a child. Focus on one flower and allow yourself to fuse with the magnificent beauty. Really taste your toast and honey. Smell the flowers in the nectar. I love the idea that bees gather nectar from flowers and herbs and then go home and make honey. We are like bees in that way. We move about, going from here to there, having

There is no end. There is no beginning. There is only the infinite passion of life.

FEDERICO FELLINI

thousands of different experiences, and learning how to cultivate our own. We take everything in, then we make our honey, our own dreams come true, our own happiness.

grace notes of happiness

Through our inner work we identify our yearnings, what we may do to fulfill our dreams. When we're acutely aware of the wonderful things happening to us all the time, cognizant of our heart's desires, we open up to an intimate connection to each new experience. Knowing what makes us feel good, what our favorite colors are, identifying the fragrances we adore, the delicious flavors we are drawn to and the sounds that lift our spirits, welcomes grace into the present.

Today well lived makes every yesterday a dream of happiness and every tomorrow a vision of hope.

SUFI PROVERB

Not life, but good life,
is to be chiefly valued.

SOCRATES

Grace notes of happiness come to us when we smell the sweet scent of hyacinths, when the sunlight illuminates the bubbles in the bath water, when we see a full moon reflected on the ocean, when we hear the sound of children laughing, when we breathe in unison to a grandfather clock ticking away, and when we hear church bells clanging. These are grace notes of happiness. When your spouse comes up behind you and gently rubs your shoulders or gives you an adoring glance from across a crowded room, when he leaves a love note on your pillow or compliments your haircut and your new blue suit, you feel these grace notes.

We feel joy when we make a pretty bed with fresh linen in anticipation of our children's visit. We enjoy setting an attractive table for a dinner sweetened by the love of our family. We take small actions every day that fill the present with goodness.

You may be seated at your writing table, pen in hand, with some freshly brewed fragrant herbal tea in a pretty cup and saucer. Before you write a letter to a friend you may pause,

Your mind can take
you anywhere.

PETER MEGARGEE
BROWN

breathe in the moment deeply, look around the room, let the flowers smile at you, let the paintings draw you into sparkling light-drenched places, let the birds sing to you, let the sea air refresh you. These are the momentary epiphanies when we have that feeling deep in our throat, "this is it." This is how authentic happiness feels. These are all grace notes of happiness. Be receptive to them, because they can come to you often, in the most unlikely places. Try to be completely present to take in as much of life's beauty as possible. When these moments come, you feel a sense of buoyancy; at the same time you experience deep inner peace. As wonderful things continue to happen, you will become more enthusiastic; you will smile easily; you will understand that you are indeed living beautifully—sublimely and happily. We can awaken to each new dawning in the realization that we are living the life of our dreams. Happiness is dreams coming true.

CHAPTER 7

participating with joy in the sorrows of the world

The best way to feel happy about yourself is when you help others.

—DEEPAK CHOPRA

Basically every being is the same. Every being has the right to be happy and to overcome suffering. There is a close con‑nection between one's self and others. Our own survival depends entirely on others, therefore, showing concern about others ultimately brings benefit to us.

—DALAI LAMA

serving others: love in action

The deepest happiness and the most life-sustaining joy come from our caring for others. When we give love we receive love in return. Our blessings multiply as we serve. Most of us were raised to feel a genuine obligation to contribute to society.

Give and take is the law of universal energy, the natural dance of life. How much we give, to whom we give, and when and where we give requires being mindful of the needs of others as well as of our own need to be helpful. When we are sensitive to other people's suffering, we grow in empathy for the concerns of those less fortunate. We awaken to the understanding that

All living things are interwoven each with the other; the tie is sacred.

MARCUS AURELIUS

giving is a privilege. There is a ricochet effect. The nurturing of others rebounds; as we give we become healed, more peaceful, happier.

Think of examples in your life of the joy you received when you loved someone unconditionally or gave anonymously to a charity or great cause. We increase our happiness when we give from a loving heart.

To understand our place in the world, we recognize that we are here to play our unique part, to use our gifts and talents to increase the light. Serving others *is* love. By giving and receiving acts of love, we sustain each other. Authentic giving transcends notions of obligation. Whenever we act out of the pure intention to truly help another human being, to be present to love someone, to lend a hand to a person in

It is better to light one small candle than to curse the darkness.

CONFUCIUS

need, known or unknown to us personally, we will feel useful and our life will have more meaning. We have been given an abundance of the earth's blessings; it feels magnificent when we give back in gratitude.

By being happy we sow anonymous benefits upon the world.

ROBERT LOUIS
STEVENSON

Going through life with outstretched arms, embracing people, concerns, and causes, being alert to a charity we want to support, as well as to a friend who needs a listening ear, is a gift we give ourselves. We will never outgrow our usefulness or our desire to be helpful.

dr. hudson's secret

Some years ago I read about finding happiness and well-being in a book with the tantalizing title *Dr. Hudson's Secret.* He enjoyed helping people anonymously. No one knew where his gifts came from. His philanthropy was unacknowledged because it was unknown. He discovered that his giving, if anonymous, would be more pure. He found that his personal sense of satisfaction was multiplied. Dr. Hudson's message never to act like a big shot, or to "follow a gift," is good to remember. The gift is always in the giving.

When you engage in fulfilling the needs of others, your own needs are fulfilled as a by-product.

DALAI LAMA

Only when we give generously of our own resources, no matter how limited, can we feel the richness of our humanity. As long as we live we have the power to choose how to give from our heart. Trust yourself. In the ups and downs of your life circumstances, there may be times when you have more time and energy to give than money. At other times you may have financial resources to contribute to the welfare of others, but less time and energy. Be true to your current reality. You will always know the right thing to do. Deepak Chopra sensibly advises, "you can only give what you have."

the world is full of profound sorrows

My aunt Betty was a pioneering missionary whose hope and focus was world peace. At times she found it hard to be deeply happy, knowing how much sadness there is in the world. While in many ways she was a cheerleader for us to do our part to try to alleviate hunger, poverty, and hatred through empathy, compassion, kindness, and love, she was acutely aware of every war, of starving children, of evil acts of hatred and discrimination. She had a conscience and was conscious. One of her main causes was world hunger.

To serve is beautiful, but only if it is done with joy and a whole heart and a free mind.

PEARL S. BUCK

Sadly, her life ended when she was only sixty-one years old. She lived on the Upper West Side of Manhattan. Walking home from the subway one night, she was brutally attacked by three youths. Rather than giving up her pocketbook that probably contained less than twenty dollars, she preached to them as though she were Gandhi, telling them that there was a better, nonviolent way. They didn't listen, and they didn't hear. She was badly beaten before they snatched her purse, leaving her semiconscious on the street. Within a week she had a fatal heart attack, was rushed to the hospital, and died.

When people are serving, life is no longer meaningless.

JOHN GARDINER

While I lived with her for a year when attending art school, I became aware of the magnitude of her compassion and caring. As a social worker, her monetary resources were meager, but her heart was full of gold. She poured out love to people all over the world, corresponding with hundreds from the far corners of the globe, encouraging and inspiring them, deeply caring for their well-being. She helped many young people obtain scholarships to universities and medical schools. Aunt Betty was someone who made the extra effort to help people live productive, meaningful lives no matter how humble.

To miss the joy is to miss all.

WILLIAM JAMES

The concerns she faced in the nineteen-fifties, sixties, and early seventies are many of the same problems we face today—overpopulation, starvation, children without families, family and child abuse, disease, drugs, poverty, crime, and violence. She was a brave woman of vision who had faith in the innate goodness of human beings. She genuinely believed she could make a difference and lead people to become more loving. The global family as a whole is not a happy one. There is sorrow at every turn—sadness because of lack of love, pain because of loss of hope, bitterness that is entrenched. What a wonderful gift we're given to be able to be of help.

accepting limitations

No matter how large our hearts or how sensitive we are to the needs of others, no life can be lived well without limits. When we wisely set limits for ourselves, doing the best we can, we live with joy and freedom. None of us will be happy if we try to be all things to all people, all the time. We have the intelligence to deliberately choose a desired course of action. With courage, resolution, and perseverance we can set our boundaries, know our limits, listen to our conscience.

To live is not to live for one's self; let us help one another.

MENANDER

OF ATHENS

letting go of guilt

Guilt is a form of self-indulgence. Rather than experiencing guilt because we feel we are not doing enough for others, we can get going and do what we can. We can make a choice and take action one way or another. When we are doing our best, genuinely trying to help others to become happier, we tend not to feel the negative emotion of guilt.

The ancient Roman poet Horace reminded us of "the man of upright life, unrestrained by guilt." Most of us have tried not to add personally to the horrors of the world. There are, however, agonizing realities we may choose to learn more about and compassionately lend our support to eradicating in whatever ways we can.

The winds of grace blow all the time. All we need to do is set our sails.

SRI RAMAKRISHNA

Never fuel a negative emotion. If you have done something wrong by omission, you will feel remorseful; learn your lesson, correct the situation, and move on. If you feel self-reproach for an inadequacy, immediately do something constructive to turn the energy into a positive affirmation.

There will always be less fortunate people who can benefit

The central purpose of each life should be to dilute the misery in the world.

KARL MENNINGER

from our care. The time to be of help is now, while we can. If we have the urge, we can go to the local hospital, a shelter, or soup kitchen and lend a hand. Far better to let your conscience guide you to do what you can than to let your energy field be polluted by the draining emotion of guilt about what you haven't done.

playing our part

We are not a one-man band. We are part of a huge well-tuned orchestra, the universe. We have to choose the instruments we feel most connected to, using our gifts and talents, playing our part to create a greater harmony. We can try to work closely with others who play various other instruments to create beautiful music. If everyone cared about one or two causes a year and made a good effort, the world's energy field would experience a more harmonious and happier shift.

Every man has owed much to others and ought to repay the kindness that he has received.

SAMUEL JOHNSON

giving gifts continue onward

We tend to think of gifts as material objects, usually in the form of money, but there are also intangible and invaluable gifts. When we express our gratitude to someone for a kindness to us, doing so is tremendously meaningful. If you are a doctor and are able to help a student go to medical school on a scholarship, think of the value of this gift. The student will also become a doctor, helping save lives, and in turn will eventually be in a position to help someone in a way similar to the way she was helped in her time of need.

The only ones among you who will be really happy are those who will have sought and found how to serve.

ALBERT SCHWEITZER

Be aware of all the ways you are giving. We often can give advice to a younger person seeking career guidance. If you are asked to help design and plant a garden in an abandoned city lot, think of the beauty people will be exposed to when they look out their windows at trees and flowering plants instead of graffiti and garbage in the street. I have a gardener friend who has a nursery in New York State. He loves to donate his time, energy, and plant materials to help people in poor city areas create gardens that they can tend with pride.

seeing need

A community in Pennsylvania needed a therapeutic hot tub for their local hospital; they had to raise ten thousand dollars. Some energetic women formed a committee, organized a fundraising event, and asked local citizens and the board members of the hospital to be sponsors and patrons and underwrite some expenses. The occasion was a sellout, and Nancy, the committee chairperson, was able to give a check to the hospital to purchase the hot tub, with some money left over.

He who wants to do good knocks at the gate; he who loves finds the gate open.

RABINDRANATH

TAGORE

volunteers

"Studies of volunteers have shown there is a benefit to performing acts of love for other people," Dr. Bernie Siegel says. "The things you do for the benefit of others not only make you feel fulfilled, they increase your chances of living a long and happy life." Mother Teresa claims not to have done great things, but rather little things with a great deal of love. When we love life, when we've tasted the inner peace and joy of sustained happiness, we want to do what we can to help relieve the pain and sorrows of the world. Erich Fromm taught that "giving is the highest expression of potency. In the very act of giving, I experience my strength, my wealth, my power . . . I experience myself as overflowing, spending, alive, hence as joyous."

When you are laboring for others, let it be with the same zeal as if it were for yourself.

CONFUCIUS

What we want from life, others also wish for. If we can share our happiness we will experience great joy. Participate with joy in the sorrows of the world. Let the precious keys to happiness in the next section open the doors to ultimate wisdom and divine love.

54 precious keys to happiness

Joy comes into our lives when we have (a) something to do, (b) someone to love, and (c) something to hope for.

—VIKTOR E. FRANKL

If you radiate love and compassion, you do receive it.

—GARY ZUKAV

precious keys

We can be happier if we choose to be—a lot happier. There will even be days of pure joy. Life is ours to celebrate. Each day we can look for miracles. We can hug a child, water a plant, kiss a lover, hold hands, create sunshine with our radiant smile, say an

> *Joy seems to me a step*
> *beyond happiness.*
>
> ADELA ROGERS
> ST. JOHN

encouraging word, stargaze, be in awe of the beauty of a mountain or the power of the ocean waves. This is our earth to embrace, appreciate, and love—fully conscious of the wonders of each moment. By concentrating our energy on increasing our inner light, we're playing our part in making the world a more sublime place.

I believe that we receive guidance from a divine universal intelligence when we compassionately make a commitment to ourselves to choose happiness. Pleasure is experienced in our outer environment; joy originates within. Love of life and others is the goal. Choosing happiness is the way. Below I've listed fifty-four precious keys to happiness. Use them as a central part of your daily practice. Choose one key a day, write it down on a piece of paper, and carry it in your wallet or put it on your desk. You may want to write a brief essay on one key a day.

Hold each key up to the light of truth, mindful of how important it is to your well-being. For example, "live each

> *Love gives us in a*
> *moment what we can*
> *hardly attain by effort*
> *after years of toil.*
>
> GOETHE

moment now" awakens us to accept what each fresh living experience brings to us without our resisting the reality of what is happening. Now is all we have control over. All the planning in the world cannot give us back this precious moment. This key alone can help us to keep our perspective, to feel the joy of being intensely present to the sparks of insights we have when we are fully conscious. Whenever we use our energy to enjoy this instant, there's happiness here; we feel joyful.

54 precious keys to happiness

- ❀ Find and pursue your passion.
- ❀ Concentrate and nurture your mind with your best thoughts and great literature.
- ❀ Recognize and honor your happier self and your inner world.
- ❀ Sustain an optimistic and positive attitude.
- ❀ Express your unique creative spirit.
- ❀ Grow in deep commitment to life.
- ❀ Create and surround yourself with beauty.
- ❀ Live each moment now.
- ❀ Do all with enthusiasm.
- ❀ Remember that ideas light the world.
- ❀ Trust that your intuition is your supreme inner intelligence.
- ❀ Let your imagination blossom.
- ❀ Live in gratitude for the gift of your life and in appreciation for the lives of loved ones.
- ❀ Cultivate self-knowledge and free will.
- ❀ Make keen use of your five senses and become a sensualist.
- ❀ Celebrate life fully with laughter and fun.
- ❀ Keep the child in you alive.
- ❀ Regularly commune with and learn from nature.

One word frees us all of the weight and pain of life. That word is love.

SOPHOCLES

Love is all we have, the only way that each can help the other.

EURIPIDES

- ❀ Stimulate your curiosity and sense of wonder.
- ❀ Realize that flowers create Paradise on earth.
- ❀ Let color celebrate your world with joy.
- ❀ Let music transport you.
- ❀ Keep a sense of humor for a sense of proportion.
- ❀ Persevere—that is the essential ingredient for all achievements.
- ❀ Practice and express kindness.
- ❀ When it rains, look for the rainbow.
- ❀ Maintain loyalty.
- ❀ Confront challenges through inner strength and courage.
- ❀ Throughout changing circumstances, seek and maintain balance and simplicity.
- ❀ Remember that order—preceding beauty—underlies all things.
- ❀ Make wise and careful choices.
- ❀ Develop your spirit energy in regular times of contemplation.
- ❀ Be a constant student of truth.
- ❀ Grow in generosity and charity.
- ❀ Practice tolerance—it is a virtue.
- ❀ Learn to forgive.
- ❀ Cultivate deep understanding.
- ❀ Cherish freedom—it makes our civilization possible.
- ❀ Grow in humility.
- ❀ Develop a crucial sense of timing.
- ❀ Let integrity and character define you.
- ❀ Be open to changing circumstances and remain flexible.

- ❀ Exercise common sense.
- ❀ Establish and maintain healthy living habits through self-discipline.
- ❀ Be patient with yourself and with others.
- ❀ Accept what you cannot change.
- ❀ Be non-judgmental.
- ❀ Sustain hope and faith.
- ❀ Practice caring as an act of grace.
- ❀ Extend compassion and empathy everywhere to everyone.
- ❀ Learn by listening.
- ❀ Find ways to serve others.
- ❀ Live each day by the Golden Rule.
- ❀ Communicate unconditional love.

Love has not age, as it is always renewing itself.

BLAISE PASCAL

All, everything that I understand, I understand only because I love. Everything is, . . . only because I love.

TOLSTOY

"love & live happy"

A small, oval, periwinkle-blue antique enamel box sits on my writing table, delighting me aesthetically as well as reminding me of my best intentions. On the top of the little box are the painted words "Love & Live Happy"—they have become my mantra. I believe this message of affirmation is the secret to happiness, inner peace, and joy.

This box is my talisman. It is sentimental, because it was a gift from Peter. When we love an object, it loves us back. I look at its beauty, I hold it in the palm of my hand, and I feel the symbolism, the sacredness of the message. When I open the lid and look at the mirror inside, I see my face. "Am I in a loving consciousness?"

Joy is always an integral part of loving. To live in love is to live in joy.

LEO BUSCAGLIA

The more loving energy we generate, the happier we will become. Pure unconditional love is a rare kind of energy that never causes pain. Love is a timeless, potent, active force of goodness. Love never dies. The more love we put into life, the greater our loving energy will radiate in all directions, spreading our own light.

When we choose happiness, we choose love. We feel vibrantly alive, in touch with our inner world, conscious of the miracle of being, here. There is always an impulse toward the ideal operating in us. I believe goodness, kindness, empathy, compassion, and forgiveness are at the heart of our essential nature, with love as the driving force. Love is our lifeline. With every heartbeat, with every breath of air we take in, life is new and fresh. Now is the only time, here is the only place, to "Love & Live Happy."

The person who truly loves does so because of a decision to be loving.

M. SCOTT PECK

Choose happiness. Let these precious keys open the door to a joyful life.

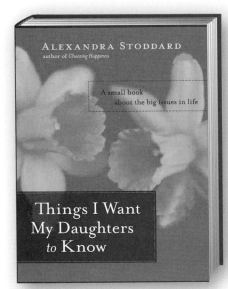